Come Grieve Through Our Eyes

Those who haven't lost a child should add *Come Grieve Through Our Eyes* to their collection, and really sit down and take time to read it. I have so many friends say to me, "I don't know what to say or do," which usually leads to them ignoring us, our child, or saying stupid things. From the moment I started reading the first chapter, right to the final chapter, I wanted to share *Come Grieve Through Our Eyes* with my friends. I know so many that I feel need to read this book, due to my experience after we lost our baby.

Come Grieve Through Our Eyes is also very insightful in helping us "pareavors" (a term introduced in this book for those who have lost a child to death) know what we can experience in this "new normal" life we now live. As I read through each chapter, many parts hit close to home and had me thinking "yes ...I too have experienced that"...."thank goodness I am not alone".... "Wow ....that hit the nail on the head".

Laura Diehl has definitely given many grieving families a voice to be heard. *Come Grieve Through Our Eyes* speaks so much truth, for both those who have lost a child, and those who want to know how to be there for us.

-Leanne Steinberger

I was in desperate need of this raw and powerful book, *Come Grieve Through Our Eyes*. At the death of my friend's daughter, I was left feeling hopeless and powerless to help. Raw and real moments revealed in the inner sanctum of grieving parents allow us "outsiders" to glimpse what these devastated parents are thinking and feeling, granting us the gift of knowing what to say and do, and what not to say and do.

This information is critical in my personal and professional life, as I attempt to support parents after the death of their child. Thank you, Laura.

-Heather Roberts,

No one can "fix" the loss of a child, or the broken parent of that child, but teaching people how to be a comfort to these parents is important. Many people have good intentions, but they don't know what to say or do, so they either clam up, or they say the wrong thing. *Come Grieve Through Our Eyes* sheds the needed light on how to help and what to say (and what not to say) to these hurting parents.

I also believe *Come Grieve Through Our Eyes* will help grieving parents themselves, and is also a tool for people who haven't lost a child, but have lost other loved ones. I know that I personally am going to be much more careful how I word things to those around me, because of the insights shared by Laura.

-Dawn Koeppen

As a pareavor myself, I was amazed at how from the very start in the preface, Laura hit the nail on the head in *Come Grieve Through Our Eyes*. It made me sad and mad, all at once, as it is true that it "becomes our duty to make people around us comfortable with our pain" as a grieving parent.

As bereaved parents, Come Grieve Through Our Eyes is a tool we can put in the hands of those around us, allowing us to begin to be set free of these kinds of damaging words and actions of those who don't mean to hurt us. We will no longer have to "become experts at fooling those around us into thinking we are strong," and will have the help and support we need.

-Kari Blackmore

I am thankful Laura has made herself so vulnerable by opening the door to her own tragic loss, while also holding the door open to be able to see into the painful journey of many other bereaved parents in *Come Grieve Through Our Eyes*. I am also thankful at how much hope she offers. Without hope, what do we have? My heart goes out to these precious parents more than ever, and I am glad that I am now equipped in knowing how to be there for them.

-Heidi Fry

I wish I would have had *Come Grieve Through Our Eyes* sixteen years ago, because I didn't know what to say, or what to do, when a good friend of mine lost her baby an hour after birth. I have personally lost two children through miscarriages, and those around me did not allow me to acknowledge my loss. While reading *Come Grieve Through Our Eyes*, I found myself crying, finally being given permission to grieve. What Laura has written will touch you in unexpected ways, and is definitely worth reading, and sharing with others.

-Alyssa Berg

Laura has crafted an invitation within *Come Grieve Through Our Eyes* in such a kind way, as to never overstimulate someone not quite ready to dive in head first, but rather to tip toe as we do, into the sea on our first trip... She patiently draws us alongside and gives us encounters through her stories with the comforters we long to be, to those in deep need of comfort.

-Hannah Linton

I love *Come Grieve Through Our Eyes,* because as a pareavor myself, I am able to see that others have felt the same things I feel. It's almost as though reading the words of these pareavors gives us the permission we desperately need to grieve, because everyone else wishes we could just move on. I believe *Come Grieve Through Our Eyes* will help family members and friends give grace to hurting parents.

-Tina Berg

In *Come Grieve Through Our Eyes*, the reader deeply feels Laura's pain, as well as the other pareavors. One of the chapters was .... a little taboo to some people, but I completely understand why it is something that needs to be in the book. *Come Grieve Through Our Eyes* is an eye-opener to exactly why and how pareavors act the same from the depth of their pain, and yet how they also differ from each other within their individual losses. *Come Grieve Through Our Eyes* is beautifully written, and as strange as it may sound, even though I cried while reading it, I loved it.

-Julie Brookhiser

I believe Laura has listened to the Holy Spirit in her writing *Come Grieve Through Our Eyes* to help others. I was definitely touched, as it gave me a glimpse into the lives of my family members who have lost their sons. I personally lost both of my parents within a year of each other, and found myself relating to many of the thoughts and emotions within the pages. I recommend *Come Grieve Through Our Eyes* to anyone who wants to understand deep loss, and how to bring comfort to those who are grieving.

-Donna Spude

I have read *Come Grieve Through Our Eyes* more than once. I have not lost a child, and it is making things so much clearer for me for those who have. Got to put it down and just hug my "babies" sometimes.

-Nysa Smith

Every grief situation is different, even for a person who has grieved over different losses. As one who has dealt with significant losses over a number of years, I have (thankfully) not dealt with the loss of a child. *Come Grieve Through Our Eyes* helped me understand a parents' unique perspective, which is a very different view from other grief situations. One has no idea how another is grieving over any loss. If you care about someone who is experiencing this kind of pain, you will want to know how to support and help them through it. *Come Grieve Through Our Eyes* is the place to begin.

-Randy Holt

When we lost my husband's brother and sister, we both said we never imagined it could hurt this bad, and our lives continued on. But when our son Josh died, neither one of us wanted life to go on. Now after losing our son, both of us say we don't know how his mom did it. *Come Grieve Through Our Eyes* is for people who truly want to understand what we are feeling. And aren't afraid of the truth.

-Kathy Pelton

Come Grieve Through Our Eyes

How To Give Comfort And Support To Bereaved Parents By Taking A Glimpse Into Our Hidden Dark World Of Grief

Laura Diehl

Copyright 2015 by Laura Diehl

Crown of Glory Ministries
PO Box 264
Janesville, WI 53547-0264

ISBN: 151861633X
ISBN-13: 9781518616334

All rights reserved under international copyright law. No part of this publication may be reproduced or transmitted in any form or by any means, electronic or mechanical, including photocopying, recording, or by any information storage and retrieval system – except for brief quotation in printed reviews - without the prior written permission of the publisher.

Printed in the United States of America.

This book is given to

_____

because I believe you to be a person of compassion who wants to know how to help bereaved parents.

This book is dedicated to bereaved parents

who are navigating their way

through the darkness of learning how to live this life

without their child.

We are bound together in heart and soul.

CONTENTS

Preface — *xvii*

Introduction: It's Not Your Fault — *xix*

1. How Does it Feel to Lose a Child? — 1
2. Does Time Heal Our Pain? — 9
3. How Do I Answer When Someone Asks "How Are You Doing"? — 13
4. Why Won't They Let Me Talk About My Child? — 19
5. Help! Does Anyone Else Have This Issue? — 25
6. How Long Does it Take to Get Past the Darkness? — 33
7. Does Losing a Child Have Any Physical Effects? — 41
8. How Do I Deal With My Child's Birthday? — 47
9. What About the Dreaded Anniversary Date? — 53
10. Why Can't People Understand That I Can't Quit Missing My Child? — 59
11. What About Melt Downs and Grief Attacks? — 65
12. What About My Other Children? — 71
13. We Lost Our Only Child — 77
14. What Does "Family" Mean to Me Now? — 83
15. Year One, Year Two, Year Three, and Beyond — 87
16. A Commercial That Blindsided Us — 93

17. How Can You Help Someone Who Lost Their Child?	103
18. Things to Avoid Saying to a Bereaved Parent	111
19. I Know How You Feel Because…	121
20. Please Don't Forget Us	129
21. Words of Hope from Bereaved Parents	135
22. The Joy of Thinking About Seeing Them Again	141
23. Choosing to Live Again	149
24. What Do I Do Now With This Information?	155

Postlude	*159*
My New Normal	*163*
About the Author	*167*
About GPS Hope	*169*
Resources	*170*
References	*171*

PREFACE

The purpose of this book is not to be morbid or to make you feel sorry for us. The purpose is to let you see inside our world. I am sure there will be times you will be uncomfortable with what you read. You might find yourself crying with some of us. And there may be times you will feel such a deep heaviness that you will want to put the book down. Go ahead. It is a very heavy subject when you begin to see the darkness we are navigating our way through. I encourage you to take advantage of the ability to set it aside and read more when you are ready; but please remember, we don't have that ability, as it is our way of life.

You will also discover how many of us have eventually found hope, and some of us have even gone on to live a full life once we figured out how to function with our unwanted "amputation" – but it takes us a few *years* to get to that point.

During that time, many people push us away as our continued pain and tears make them uncomfortable and we are told we should be over the death of our child by now. (Just stab us in the heart and twist the knife please....) So we learn to wear a mask and say everything is fine. This book is a truthful view of that "fine" behind our masks.

What you will be reading was written by grieving parents. Most of this book was put together by copying comments from social media sites for grieving parents, thus making it a *safe* place to spill our hearts out – to each other. You have a right to your silent opinions about our gaping wounds that eventually scab over but never fully heal. But unless you have walked in our shoes, please don't judge us, especially to our faces or on places like our Facebook walls. Every one of us will say we hope and pray you *never* have to join this unwanted nightmare "club" of grieving parents.

Thank you for choosing to try and come into our world. It means a lot to us...more than we can say.

INTRODUCTION

It's Not Your Fault

Many well-meaning family and friends of grieving parents will make an attempt to help those parents through the most difficult trauma a person can face in life. I am sorry to say that very few will succeed by truly being there in the way that bereaved parents need them, especially the farther out the death of their child becomes.

Several will start out with good intentions, but they soon fall off the grief wagon, feeling like the parent should be past the darkness and getting on with life. Or the busyness of their own life keeps them from seeing the pain, confusion, and isolation of that parent over time.

Most will fail. When I say "most", I mean 95%. I am not talking about those who stop by with food, or give a phone call in that first month. I am talking about beyond that time, when these hurting parents need someone the most, months and even years down the road.

Perhaps you have already experienced one of these failures. Maybe you know what it's like to make a commitment with deep passion to be there for a friend who has tragically lost a child, only to realize at some point your life went on as normal, and you never really followed through.

Maybe you have suffered this kind of burning guilt more than once. Maybe you feel like no matter how hard you try, you're just never going to know how to really be there for a grieving friend or family member, especially one who has lost a child.

Does any of this sound familiar?

Don't feel bad - you're not alone, and it's not your fault.

The reason for your frustrated efforts is not a lack of willpower, it's not lack of sympathy, and it's not a moral failing on your part.

The reason why you can't seem to know how to be there for that grieving person who needs you is really quite simple, and even easy to fix. What has held you back is not knowing how to act on your compassion - nobody has shown you the whole story. You don't know why we isolate ourselves, because we don't have words to even begin to describe the suffocating darkness we find ourselves hurled into with the wrongness of having our child leave this earth before we do. You don't have an open door to see behind the mask we grieving parents are eventually forced to put on for others. It becomes our "duty" to make the people around us comfortable with our pain, and we become experts at fooling those around us into thinking we are strong, and that at some point we are okay and have pretty much forgotten about our child, leaving them in our past like everyone else has.

Let that soak in. What that means is that as grieving parents, we have done a great job at shutting others out of our world of darkness, confusion, and suffocating pain. Unless you have lost a child, you probably have no idea how many tears still fall years later, and how painful it is to feel like no one cares or remembers that our child once lived on this earth.

All you need is for a bereaved parent to be willing to open that door for you to see the raw and real pain, and then you can have something that goes beyond condolences and sympathy. You can have compassion at a level that will truly help us, and be a strength to us, at our deepest level of need.

It's really that simple. But maybe not obvious.

Every true empathizer to a grieving parent involves themselves in learning about their world, and being willing to help carry their pain.

Sometimes that's not obvious because we think there are people who were just born with a greater capacity to walk with others through tragic and traumatic times.

They weren't.

At one time, everyone who is in that 5%, who sticks with and truly helps a bereaved parent, started right where you are right now.

There's no reason holding you back from being part of that 5%.

And there's even better news: you can "figure it out" faster, better, and easier than those who came before you because this book you hold in your hands, *Come Grieve Through Our Eyes*, opens the door to the raw and real life behind the masks of dozens of grieving parents.

If you can read, then you can know how to help us!

Maybe you feel like you've tried to be there for someone grieving a deep loss before, but it just never worked out. So you're probably fairly skeptical about some book being the answer to knowing how to help them.

But this book is different. That's because it covers specific issues grieving parents are forced to deal with. These are actual words coming from parents who are facing day-to-day life after the death of their child.

When you read *Come Grieve Through Our Eyes* you will discover:

- What you must know before stepping in to help a bereaved parent
- Understand exactly how anyone can console a grieving parent without making their pain even worse – it's not as tough as you think (and it's probably different than you think, too)
- The secret to giving a grieving parent almost instant relief from their emotional pain
- How to know what to say and not to say (the normal clichés for grief don't work for grieving parents, and greatly intensifies our pain, darkness, and confusion)

The subject of death itself can be heavy, and the death of one's child, no matter the age, is considered by most experts to be one of, if not the heaviest and darkest grief to be faced. [1] I am not calling attention to this information to diminish the grief of other forms of loss. This is an area that probably causes the most tension with those who have not lost a child, but have experienced a significant loss in their lives. Comparing the pain of our grief does no one any good. However, I think it is important to validate the fact that parents who have lost a child through death, have a weight that is extremely heavy...heavier than most will experience in this life.

As a parent who has experienced this horrific event, I found myself trying to think of a word to describe what I felt, and the only thing that came to me is *death*—the pain of my own death. A part of us dies along with our child.

This got me thinking. A widow or widower is someone who has lost their spouse; an orphan is someone who has lost their parents. Since it is acknowledged that losing a child is the worst loss a person can go through in life, then why isn't there a word for us?

I have thought and prayed long and hard on this. One day I sat down and listed all the words possible for parents, grief, bereaved, children, etc. to see what I could put together as a word for a grieving or bereaved parent.

That is how I made the word being introduced in this book: PAREAVOR. A pareavor is a parent who has lost a child through death. How did I come up with this?

> *"Pa" comes from the word parent: a person who is a father or mother; a person who has a child (Merriam-Webster)*
>
> *"Reave" comes from the word bereave. The meaning of the actual word "reave" (which the word bereave comes from) is: to plunder or rob, to deprive one of, to seize, to carry or tear away (Merriam-Webster).*
>
> *"Or": indicating a person who does something (Wiktionary)*

This sounds like a pretty good description of what happens when a child dies, no matter the age of the child. So a "pareavor" is a parent who has been deprived of their child who was seized and torn away from them through death.

You will find pareavor being used throughout the book. It might feel a bit awkward at first, but I believe it won't take long for it to become a natural word that makes sense and you will understand its usefulness and need. (It is definitely easier than constantly saying, "a person who has lost their child", or "a grieving parent", or "a bereaved parent.") Pareavors. That is who we are.

Before we go any further, I want to acknowledge those pareavors who may not have actually given birth to their child, but he or she was their child through adoption. Too many people (including other pareavors at times, unfortunately) have a lack of understanding, believing that these grieving parents can't experience the same depth of pain.

I disagree, and let me explain why. I came into our marriage with Becca. She was not Dave's biological child, but his love, care, and protection of her was the exact same as our other four children. I watched him grieve the death of *our* daughter, and still do.

Dave adopted Becca as his own when she was two years old, giving him a beautiful front row seat of Romans 8:15, "…you received God's Spirit when he adopted you as his own children. Now we call him, "Abba, Father" (NLT). Adoption is a covenant that God honors and takes very seriously. I believe, based on this scripture and others, that there is an intertwining which happens, between a parent and child who is adopted, causing the same level of connection as if that child had been conceived and birthed by those parents.

So as you read this book, even if you read statements from grieving parents that seem to contradict what I just wrote, please remember they are speaking from their own place of pain, and that most of them are not trying to say parents who adopted their child do not go through this. They just do not specifically qualify their statements with a disclaimer for adoptive parents. I hate to even be writing all of this, out of concern of singling out pareavors who adopted their child as if they need to be validated. But unfortunately, many of them do. If you are one of them, I am sorry you have this added dimension to your grief that you should not have, and I stand with you.

And to all of us, if you don't know already, you will soon find out: Grief needs *lots* of grace!

There is really only one place pareavors can go to safely share and vent their raw and real emotions, and that is other pareavors; those who have experienced the same blackness, confusion, and turmoil. That is why this book was written by pulling out quotes from several social media sites set up specifically for grieving parents. Before each quote, you will find the initials of the parent who wrote it, as in the following example:

> *D.C.: Sometimes others put conditions on our grief from child loss. "You lost a baby? So, just have another one and everything will okay." "Your child was an adult. Why are you living so much in the past? At least you had all of those years together." "Your child was sick. Why would you want him/her to continue suffering?" "Think of how awesome it is having your child in heaven! Why are you crying so much?" And, on and on it goes. People mean well when they say things, BUT what they don't understand is there is nothing -- absolutely nothing -- that takes away the pain of losing a child! Our child was part of our heart, part of our soul, part of the very air we breathe, and we will forever miss our child. That doesn't mean we're living in the past, or that we don't understand the beauty of heaven, or that we don't understand how important it is for life to go on. It simply means we will forever miss our child and nothing will change that!*

Allow me to share a quick summary of my own loss. Our oldest daughter, Becca, had bone cancer at the age of three. She had her left leg amputated and went through nine months of chemotherapy. What saved her life then is what caused her death 26 years later. One of the chemo drugs caused heart damage, which showed up majorly as a teenager. Constant complications the last decade of her life put her in and out of the hospital, including almost losing her during her pregnancy and delivery, having open heart surgery to repair a valve, getting a heart pump (called a VAD – Ventricular Assist Device), a stroke, and other events that caused a dozen ambulance rides and three medical helicopter flights. She became too ill to even be put on the heart transplant list, and on October 11, 2012, her heart finally gave out and she went home to dance with Jesus on two legs and a forever healed heart. (If you are interested in the full story, it can be found on our website at www.gpshope.org.)

As I was putting this book together, I found myself coming under the heaviness of the words of these hurting parents. And as I already mentioned in the preface, I am sure at times you will have the same feeling. In fact, there may be times you need to put the book down, because you just can't handle reading any more of our pain. I encourage you to put the book down and take the break from it you need. However…please come back. You have the luxury of walking away. A luxury we do not have, which is one of the issues most people around us fail to realize. I have tried to balance this possible heaviness out by ending each chapter with "Words of Grace and Hope." These are quotes from pareavors speaking about the life and hope they have eventually discovered after the death of their child.

You might want to get a pen and a highlighter to keep with *Come Grieve Through Our Eyes* to mark those things the Lord emphasizes to you personally as you go through the book. Plus, it will help you to be able to quickly refer back and remind yourself of these things should the need arise farther down the road.

And before you go any further, I would like to make a request that you say a prayer, asking the Holy Spirit to speak to you as you immerse yourself into our world to show you what He wants you to see, and to do what He wants you to do.

Done? Then let's get started. I open the door and invite you into our world, the hidden world of a pareavor.

CHAPTER 1

||||||||

How Does it Feel to Lose a Child?

Some people (myself included) describe the death of a child like an amputation. The daughter we lost at age 29 lived 26 of those years with only one leg. It was amputated when she was only three years old, due to bone cancer. So we have experience with what living with an amputation is like.

You have to learn how to live and function with a part of you missing. It can be done. But unless you have had to learn how to live day-to-day with an amputation, you don't realize or understand the many things in life it affects.

For example, there was the issue of our daughter's shoes. She had a prosthesis, which helped her live a more normal life growing up. Her right foot would grow, but the left foot stayed the same size until she outgrew the actual leg and a new one had to be made. What size shoe do you buy when your child literally has two different size feet, since one grows and the other does not? How badly will it make her stumble, having one shoe a size too big on one foot?

To go swimming, she would have to take off her fake leg and hop on her one real leg to get into the pool as quickly as possible, in order to keep from being stared at so much. Her towel would be used to cover up her fake leg lying on the ground or lounge chair. And when she was done, she would hop quickly on her one leg from the pool back to her fake leg (which was scary to watch, knowing how slippery those surfaces could be) dry off her stump, and put her leg on without calling too much attention to herself.

These are just a couple of examples of how different our lives were, raising a child with an amputation.

Yes, an amputation is a good description to help people understand what it is like to lose a child through death. But there is another one that actually seems even better to me.

It is like a hole in the heart that cannot heal. This is the closest true description of child loss that I have heard. It affects everything you do in the very core of your being. I don't even know how to elaborate on this. Just take whatever that means to you, and then intensify it about 100 times.

But don't take my word for it. Here are what other parents have to say in answer to the question, "How does it feel to have your child die?"

> D.C: Try and imagine how much you miss your child when they go away to summer camp or something similar, then try to imagine NEVER seeing them again. Not just that but no contact at all. No phone calls, no letters, no nothing. And then add into that no one really wants to talk about him, just move on and leave, well... roughshod. That is child loss!
> K. H.: It's a painful canyon so deep there is no end.
> C.C.N: It is an amputation without anesthesia.
> V.M.:... like waiting to exhale.
> A.H.: It's so hard when every single aspect of your life is a reminder ...bittersweet
> M.W.D.: The pain is just totally indescribable; most people couldn't imagine !!!!!
> B.W.: I agree it will never heal, it just has some scar tissue over it.
> M.B.: My heart is so broken; hard to believe it can still beat.
> V.M.: I hold my 2 sons close to my heart and each of them are in it, but in different ways. I don't love one more than the other I just love them individually because they are not the same person. Then there's the hole in between them where my middle son used to be. I still hold all that love in its place, but it's not the same as loving him when he was alive. That hitch you get in

> *your throat when they've made you proud, the way your heart skips a beat when they've accomplished a first, it's gone, it's not there, it's like it's on hold but it can never be let out again.*
> *S.R.: Nobody likes to feel broken, but......there is no other way to describe those who are living the daily pain of child loss. There is no quick fix, no sure-fire remedy, nothing that is a guaranteed-for-life solution. Why? Because a child is part of our own heart -- we are connected at the very soul of our being and when our child is separated from us, we are broken. There's nothing to be ashamed of in saying that. Maybe it's time to recognize that the reality of child loss is we will never be complete again -- not in this life -- because our child left a very distinct hole in our heart.*

During my first year of grieving the death of Becca, God showed me something that was truly amazing, and explained specifically why a mother's grief is so intense. I shared this in my book *When Tragedy Strikes* and would like to share it here as well.

> Three months after Becca's death, I had the following revelation. This brought so much understanding to my grief as a mom that I can't even put it into words. It has been a *huge* part of my understanding why I am so very connected to my children, and why we as mothers feel the death of our child so deeply for the rest of our lives. My hope and prayer is that it does the same for you!
>
> 1/18/12: 1) I am a spiritual being in a physical body 2) I *do* feel much closer to the reality of heaven and that part of the spiritual realm now 3) death is a spiritual event, a crossing over into the spirit realm. Because she is a part of me, it was within my womb that she received her spirit. (WHOA! Now there is a Selah! I was carrying her spirit within me as I

carried her as a fetus!) The death of her body and the leaving of her spirit affect me in a way they affect no one else. Okay, Holy Spirit, you've got to show me some scriptures to base this on. It makes perfect sense, but I need to see confirmation in Your Word! That is why a mom's identity is wrapped up in her children!

God immediately gave me the following examples to confirm this revelation, which I also recorded.

Judges 13:7 Samson's mother was to be consecrated herself because of the child she carried—she was held to a Nazarite vow while carrying him. Psalm 22:10… "From my mother's womb you have been my God." Psalm 58:3 makes me realize it is a pure spirit that is not separated from God yet by sin! Jeremiah 1:5 "Before I formed you in the womb I knew you…" Spirit to spirit? Hosea 12:3 "he took his brother by the heel in the womb, and in his strength he struggled with God." Was the fighting in Rebecca's womb a spiritual battle? The spirits of these two boys fighting each other? Genesis 25—two nations? Luke 1:15 John was filled with the Holy Spirit in his mother's womb, which means he had his own spirit for God to fill. Luke 1:41, 44 John's spirit recognized the Son of God in Mary's womb while inside Elizabeth's womb! It was his spirit inside of her—not his fleshly body obviously (or his soul) that recognized the Spirit of God so close to him.

Then I wrote the following as I heard God speak it to me:

> *Laura, a mother who has nurtured (carried) the spirits of her children is going to be greatly entwined in her children's spiritual lives, so greatly entwined that only I can separate them—just as My Word can separate the joint and morrow, the thoughts and intents of the heart. Your children are not "who you are," but they are part of the trunk of the tree, which is greater than the branches. They spring from the very roots, and for many it takes Me to separate the two! You are okay. Part of your trunk has been chopped out and there is a bleeding that is taking place, with the healing in process. A sealing of that wound. It will be forever scarred, and sometimes may leak sap, but it will heal and is still a strong tree! (With many fruitful, flourishing branches.) This wound in the tree causes it to pull from the roots to a new depth, never before known to that tree. Any time a child goes through trauma, the mother is greatly affected. You have been chopped many, many times. This last time was a blow to previous chopping's, which is why it has been so traumatic and the healing will take longer. But the character and the shade you will provide by digging in so deeply to be rooted and grounded in My love will be like no other, and beautiful to more than you will ever know in this lifetime. Yes, some will not understand or see the beauty, but I do—I created you, knowing what every blow would become in you. I see nothing but beauty as You allow me to do My work. Yes, My child, there is deep healing for deep wounds. Continue to rest in Me through this process.*

So You are telling me that I can't just receive this revelation and be on a new level, soaring past the pain because it is a process I must go through to be able to connect with others when they go through a process of pain and grief? I don't like it, don't want it, but I will accept it, because I know You *are* love, and it must be in Your love for me that You are doing it this way. I wanted to have the pain be lifted... But I will be thankful for the revelation. I know it will be used greatly in the process of my healing. Thank You. I want to live my life by the roots that cannot be seen instead of the tree that can be. The roots are who I really am. They are what I come from and am connected to, to make the tree what it is.

Wow! Every time I read this, I am amazed at how powerful it is. Thank You, Father God, for Your love that never ends, and for the way You are so very willing to comfort us and give us wisdom and new revelation!

So how does it feel to lose a child? All of us who have been hurled into a life-long membership in this unwanted club hope and pray you never have to find out.

Words of Grace and Hope

L.H.: *Life does change. You will never get over the loss, but there is hope, and you do have better days. I lost my son in 2013, each day is a new day. Some better than others, but Gods mercies are new every morning.*

T.B.K.: *It's a tragedy because it's not fair and it's not natural to have a child go before you. This October 31st will be 10 years since my son, my only child, died in his sleep from sepsis due to MRSA at the age of 25... Losing a child splits you in two. You are never whole again and that's ok. You are like a great oak tree, and the loss of a child is like lightning that strikes the oak, splitting and burning the bark, leaving the strong tree still alive but damaged forever. The tree doesn't die, it can't; it's needed to go on and provide life for so many others who love it and depend on the tree. Going on with your life, honors your child. You keep their memory alive...*

CHAPTER 2

|||||||

Does Time Heal Our Pain?

"Time does not heal the pain of child loss. Time simply puts distance between our initial shock and pain, and where we are now. Time adds fear to the bereaved parent's life; fear that we will forget our child's voice, forget our child's smell, forget the details of our child's face, forget what it felt like to hold our child. No, time does not heal the pain of child loss. Our healing will come when we see our child again in heaven, and so we cling tightly to that hope as we pass through the long, dark valley of time." - Anonymous

Time alone does not heal our shattered hearts. It's not time that heals, but what you do in that time. In the cemetery where Becca is buried, there is a section of babies and infants that were born in the 70's and 80's. Almost half of those graves continue to have fresh decorations, 40 years later.

When stated how time does not heal our pain, most of the responses on social media are things like, "That is so very true", or "Thank you for putting into words how I feel." Here are some actual responses to the thought of how time does not bring a healing to their shattered hearts.

A.M.H.: The whole dimension of "time" doesn't even seem to exist/apply when you've lost a child...that's why "others" think we should be able to get past it & also why we know we never will.

S.C.: I used to believe I would "get over it" because I heard people talking as if that was the case. Never happened. My daughter only lived for a few hours 41 years ago. Not one day has ever gone by that I haven't thought about her. Having other

children didn't change it...actually it probably increased the amount of thoughts I had about her for awhile. (This seems to truly surprise people...as though one child could ever replace another....)

L.S.: The worst is people pretending the child didn't exist in the name of sparing your feelings.

A.M.: You can never get over it or replace them. My son was stillborn a week before I was due 2 years ago, I have since had a daughter and she didn't replace him. I think about him every day.

K.K.S.: You are soo right! My child was 50, but I don't think I'll ever get over it!

S.S.D.: My (child) was 2 days old when she passed. I never got to hold her or tell her I loved her. She would have turned 40 on January 18th. The pain is still here every day.

L.A.: I lost my 16 yr old son 10 yrs ago, and the pain is still there as much today as the night he was killed. He's the first thing I think of when I wake and the last when I go to bed. I miss him so much...

E.W.: It's difficult to find something to be thankful for when all you want is to be with your child. Total meltdowns every day, no. But a hundred mini meltdowns and tears flowing daily. Happiness never comes without guilt. Moving forward? Sorry, I don't know what that is, even eight years later. I know this experience is different for everyone, but for me, nothing will be "better," only different. I miss you (daughter) everyday more intensely than the last.

R.M.: You never forget you just learn to live with it.

C.A.T.E.: Today would've been my sons 24th birthday. I lost him when he was 17. It's not fair. And I think the pain of not having him here is getting worse. I have also lost my mom, my aunt and my grandmother. After (son) passed, it took a toll on everyone. So I don't have hardly any family. And nobody brings (son) up. Nobody says his name. It hurts. I don't know if they are afraid it's going to hurt me or if they just don't care! I am only 48. But I feel like I'm 80.

Does Time Heal Our Pain?

> J.F.S.: *Almost three years since my beautiful (daughter) has been gone..still miss her every second but the meltdowns are less frequent.*
>
> L.H.T.: *I always ask myself where the deep, debilitating, agonizing, bring you to your knees, vomiting, sighing, sorrow went. For over a year this was a daily occurrence. Then around 13 months there was a shift. A shift in the sorrow. It became a yearning, a wanting a missing. It was softer. It eased. It does return in waves or spurts but they don't last as long and the intensity is not as deep. I really don't know why or how. Someone told me you get used to it. And maybe that is it.*

Here is a word of encouragement by a pareavor, followed by just a few responses.

> *How do I know that I'm beginning to deal with the reality of child loss a little bit better? This is a question every parent of child loss asks. When you can get up in the morning and find something to be thankful for. When you can make it through one day without having a total meltdown. When you no longer feel the urgent need to visit the cemetery every day. When you can smile and not feel guilty about it. These are some of the ways that will let you know you're moving forward in your grief from child loss. Of course, you'll always miss your child with every ounce of your being BUT it's good to know that there can be moments of joy, too. God bless every parent and family of child loss today with some special moments of hope and joy!*
>
> E.G.: *Guess I'm not dealing with it any better yet. Who knows if I ever will.*
>
> V.W.: *Thanks for that. I look forward to when that day comes. My grief is wearing me down. It overwhelms me each day and has since Oct. 27 2014. Some days better than others. Today not good, so it made me feel good to read that. Thanks!!*
>
> C.S.: *It is 3yrs i lost my youngest son and by far this is the worst year yet. I will never get to that point*
>
> J.G.: *2nd & 3rd years were the worst for me - My daughter was 28 when she died and will be gone 15 years this July - Still*

have some really bad days and I still say her name at *least 3 times a day. Your life is changed but goes on.*

Time…I hated the thought of hitting the 5 year mark, the 10 year mark…and would feel a stabbing pain that could take my breath away at the thought of being 20 years "away" from Becca. How will I be able to live, getting farther and farther away from her? (Something many other bereaved parents say and feel as well.)

God so graciously showed me something about my thought in this area of "time," to change my perspective. I am not getting farther away from Becca, I am getting closer to her. Each day I remain on this earth is a day I am closer to my own departure, which means I am actually getting closer to her, not farther away!

Perspective can change everything. But it cannot be "forced" on a person. It can only be gently presented as a thought, allowing those in deep grief to take it and make the change in how they see it.

Words of Grace and Hope

E.B.: Every day brings us another day closer to that sweet reunion day. I write letters to my children every night and start them with these words: Another day ends and it brings us one day closer.

S.T.T.: 6 years ago we lost my daughter to suicide. I could barely get out of bed and when I did, I didn't want to live. We had a wonderful life before she died and I wanted that life back. I missed me and I didn't think I could ever get me back, so I was in the mindset that I was waiting to die. I didn't want to die, I just didn't want to live without my daughter. Slowly with time and other bereaved parents, my attitude changed. I learned that life was still worth living even though I felt like I had died. I have days that are not all filled with sadness, I have found a way to let joy back in. I am where I am at because of other bereaved parents who showed me that living a life was still possible.

CHAPTER 3

How Do I Answer When Someone Asks "How Are You Doing"?

This is a very "hot" topic with grieving parents, with thoughts all over the place. This is one area the masks come off very quickly, because it is the one we put on the most often.

We have to do an immediate in depth examination to be able to answer the simple question, "How are you?"

- First, are you asking about this exact moment, or as a whole? This can cause me to have two completely different answers.
- Are you asking because you really want to know, or is it more of a greeting because you don't know what else to say, and you want or expect a quick answer of "fine" so you can move on?
- Are you just the clerk at the store who is using it more as a greeting, and I really shouldn't unload on you in sarcasm and pain, no matter how I am feeling at the moment?
- Are you a safe person to give a truthful answer to?

At this point, I am exhausted going through all the options in my head, determining it is the easiest on both me and the one asking to give a generic pat answer, so you probably won't get the truth.

Here is a question I saw posted in social media about this subject:

"I never know how to answer the question, 'how are you doing?' Any advice on how to respond?"

There were 278 replies within 4 hours! I told you it is a hot topic. I have done my best to give you a good representation of those replies. I would say well over half of them were things like, "I'm hanging in there", "taking one day at a time", or "I'm doing okay".

> B.B.: *After our son died, one of the most sage pieces of advice I received was "Know your lines." By that, my friend was suggesting that I have a few responses ready for when people would inevitably ask that question. The sad truths are that not everyone who asks really wants to know, not everyone who asks can handle an honest reply, and I didn't always want to have the conversation. For me, my line is "We are putting one foot in front of the other." Occasionally I will say "One breath and then another," if it feels right.*
>
> A.B.: *I always answer "I'm alive, I'm dressed, I'm out of bed, I'm working, and taking it day by day the best I can". Just be honest.*
>
> K.B.: *... my response is usually, "I'm doing okay". To me, doing okay and being okay are two completely different things. You can be doing okay, but it doesn't mean your heart isn't completely broken.*
>
> D.G.: *...I typically answered hanging in there. A lady at church caught on and asked, "by a rope or a thread?"*
>
> D.H.S.: *"I'm breathing, and that's a pretty good feat right now". I honestly forget to breathe sometimes.*
>
> M.R.P.: *" I don't know how to answer either. I just say ok because I don't think people really want to know how I'm doing.*
>
> E.H.: *I am a Christian, and I wish people had just simply said: "How can I pray for you?" Because then I could have answered to the degree I felt I could confide in the individual asking. Honestly, the thing I most wanted to say was: "My child is dead. How do you THINK I'm doing???" ... I would have liked it if people had just simply asked "How are you*

feeling?" and then would SIMPLY LISTEN, *and then say something like "I cannot imagine how you must be feeling. I am so terribly sorry this happened." But the chances of real people actually doing that, without giving condescending advice or judging your grieving process in an unhelpful way is slim.*

D.L.: (written on a poster picture) People always tell me I look sad and tired. I know I look sad and tired. I am sad and tired.

J.M.P.: …I usually turn to humor. It helps me cope and it's the way I was raised. My grandma used to say "I'm vertical and ventilating." I often use that. It makes them think for a minute and it pretty adequately describes how I feel most days.

G.S.: I just say I am doing good ....if I go in to it I might breakdown & they do not know how to handle that... I think the tears scare them...they just do not know what to do... But u know, I don't either.

M.M.: … I answer the same way for me based on my beliefs. I'm getting by with Gods help.

M.T.: I say good, because if people knew the truth they wouldn't ask anymore! What am I gonna say.... It's been 21 months since I last saw my daughter alive and life sucks now!!!

L.P.P.: I just say fine because the very few times I've broke down and told the truth they didn't want to hear it!! So unless it's a really bad day and I can't hold the tears back I just lie and say I'm fine!!

H.F.: tell them the truth. "Not good. Each day is a struggle." I'm sure people avoid me at times because they need the old me back. That will never happen.

C.K.: If they know of your loss, I think it's healing to tell them the truth of how you're doing at the time. Speaking of our loss and the one we've lost can be more cathartic than you may think. When people ask me, sometimes I just respond with, 'I could sure use a hug.'

J.P.W.: Taking it one day at a time...sometimes just moment to moment. I always thank them for asking and hug them. Their courage to even ask that question makes me want to hug them to show my appreciation for them not just avoiding me

D.A.A.: ... *Sometimes I would say, I feel okay--right this second. (Meaning ask me in two minutes and you might get a different answer.)*

M.B.: I always just say "who knows" because I don't even know.

S.M.: ...I'm not okay right now, but it's just too difficult to talk about.

L.M.: I tell people "I'm here..." Most understand what that means. I guess I would rather people said, I am thinking of you... I am thinking of your beloved son."

J.M.M.: I always thank them for asking, then I reply, One day at a time one step at a time. I also tell them the other children are doing well. (I always make sure they know how much I appreciate them asking, because people lack compassion these days and it needs to be appreciated when it is shown.)

P.G.S.: Seven years later I still say "I have my good days and my bad days". Sometimes people are surprised but it's the truth.

D.T.: What can I do for you? Let's go for a walk. NOT how are you doing. ... I have lost both of my children. I would have much rather have had a hug with no words. Because there's nothing one can say that will matter.

K.L.: I always said "fine". I figured it wasn't a real invitation to share the pain. Most people ask how you are to be polite. They don't really want to know how you feel.

J.O.B.: I always answer honestly.... If it's a good day, I'll say it....bad day, the same. I remember to always say "Thank you for asking" so that they're aware that it matters to me that they have asked. If they inquired out of concern, they'll respond compassionately. Those simply going through the motions deserve to know our feelings are genuine and need to be answered with a true response, not with the simple "I'm okay" answer.

J.M.N.D.: All is well with my soul. I'm thankful for life it is still a precious gift. n how are u doing?

C.I.B.: "I'm ok." And "I'm alright" even though I'm crumbling and aching inside when I say it.

M.M.A.: I hate having to say it when I don't really feel it, but it's easier. I usually just say that I'm doing pretty good.

> *D.G.R.: I always answered honestly. Those who really cared and could handle the truth would encourage a person to talk. Those who can't handle the truth would change the topic. "How are you" is such a common phrase, but often people don't really wait for an answer. I won't ask anyone that question if I'm not prepared to listen. Last fall I went into a convenience store that I go to quite often. There was the usual "hi" and "how are you". On this particular day the cashier said something like "OK, I guess". Of course I couldn't leave it at that and asked a few more questions. It turned out that it was the month that would be her son's one year date of his death. I guess I kind of went off topic a bit from this post, but I just wanted to take the opportunity to remind people of how important it is to listen to someone's answer if you ask that question.*

In reading through all of these responses, you may have noticed three things:

1. There is bitterness and sarcasm involved in the pain of people asking how we are doing, and not really caring.
2. In the realness behind the mask, we are acknowledging that what we say is only a surface answer of the depth we truly feel, which is pointless to try to put into words.
3. It is all based on our perspective. Some of us have the view of, "How can you even bother asking? You don't really care. And if you did care, you would know and wouldn't have to ask." While others of us have the view of, "Even though I may not be able to give you a full, truthful answer, I appreciate you asking, because it shows me at least you care." And some of us have both views, depending on the moment you ask the question.

So do you ask, or not ask? My suggestion would be, only ask if you are sincerely concerned, and want to allow us an opportunity to express the truth of the depth of our pain.

Or instead of asking how we are doing, just let us know you are thinking of us and our child (and also praying for us, if you are) and maybe give us a hug, if appropriate.

Sorry we have put everyone around us on eggshells. Please love us and pray for us. We are fragile and very broken, just like those eggshells.

Words of Grace and Hope

C.H.: Without the hope of heaven, we get lost in a drowning sea of grief. We will never understand why our child had to leave us too soon -- that part of child loss will always be a mystery. But, with heaven to look forward to, we know we can make it through today.

D.B.P.: I still have sadness, and many more things in life have a greater meaning to me. Number one is my relationship with God, number 2 is my relationship with those I love. These are the only really important things in life, the rest is baseless, material things that are to be used and left behind. One day I will see my son again; for now he is with Jesus, and that's good enough for me...

CHAPTER 4

||||||||

Why Won't They Let Me Talk About My Child?

As pareavors, we have a need to keep our child's memory alive. One of the ways we do that is to talk about our child. Other people eventually don't talk about them, and so we don't hear their names come up in conversations anymore. And if the child was young, not very many people had a chance to know our child, so the conversations about them are even fewer. Often, the lack of hearing people acknowledge our child's life intensifies our need to talk about them, which people around us often do not understand.

Child loss is a trauma - a heartbreaking trauma - and parents need to be able to talk freely about their child. Quite often they are shut off by others who don't want to listen by changing the subject abruptly, or simply saying, "You're living too much in the past."

One of the best ways others can help is to simply be good listeners. Allow parents to tell their story as often as they feel the need, and that includes being okay with any tears.

Here is what grieving parents have to say about this subject to other pareavors.

> *D.D.S.: I talk about all his positive points so that I can just speak his name.*
> *C.T.P.: I have always been able to talk about the tragic way we lost our son. It helped me with the grieving process; however, my husband can't always talk about it. Everyone deals with the loss differently. I feel the need to talk about it. I can tell people*

get upset hearing my story, it brings them to tears. I think they are more uncomfortable hearing it than I am telling it. I always apologize to them, lol.

T.A.T.: I can talk all day everyday about my beautiful daughter, it keeps her memory alive

S.V.: I play it in my head every day, over & over, what happened from day one when my baby boy got sick. I remember every single detail. I only tell people that don't know what really happened. My husband & daughter & I are always reminiscing on all the cute things my baby did or things we always said to him. Miss him like crazy

S.T.: I talk about my son all the time. I know it makes some people uncomfortable but I need to keep my son's memory alive.

M.G.K.: I'm keeping (daughter's) memory alive....if it's the last thing I do

R.C.: I hate being told to "move on" like I can simply forget or let go of the memories. I understand that time does not stand still and I am not living in the past. Instead I'm embracing the love I shared and will eternally be grateful for the moments we had.

L.W.Y.: I was very careful not to post on f/b a whole lot about (son) but about 3 mos. after his suicide, I posted his photo and wrote how much I was missing him. A "friend" told me I needed to stop dwelling on his death and move on. Needless to say, she's no longer a friend.

L.D.:... I had a person scream and yell at me, questioning me about why I had left (daughter's) bedside to go to the store. This person had not been in the family very long, and the rage with which he vented, shocked and confused me. Another one that got me, was, "at least you got to have a child, I could never have one and that's worse". Or, "your daughter is the closest I ever got to having a child of my own, and we all miss her!" I'm still trying to find the comfort in that statement; after 6 years, I still don't see it! Reading back on what I just wrote, I know now why I rarely cry or talk out loud about my most precious and loved (daughter)! Why bother, based upon the preview of what was to come. I just shut down and let the grief and anger eat me up from the inside..... Thank you for this post..... I think I just unraveled a mystery that will help me get well!

C.E.: Our stories are who we are and who our lost children are. The trauma of child loss does not happen in a vacuum but is a lifelong tragedy that bereaved parents live through daily.

J.S.M.: I will forever talk about my son and keep his spirit alive. There have been some people tell me I need to get things back to normal and then I ask what is normal because my normal will never be normal. My son has been in Heaven for 2 years and 5 1/2 months. My heart is forever broken

M.M.R.: I have wonderful friends and family who will listen!!!

C.V.: I have a tattoo for my son in an obvious place. You can't look at me without seeing his name.

D.F.: ... finding people who are open to listen is important, or it can just add to the trauma.

M.S.: My daughter doesn't like talking with me about her brother and it bothers me immensely. I need to talk about my son.

B.E.W.: My partner doesn't like to talk about our baby, neither do others. I never used to, but I like to now

J.E.: Love to talk about (son) and for people to talk about him. Love and miss him so much.

K.W.: Most people are uncomfortable with talking about it for fear you will get upset. It's unfortunate. Pretty much any activity I do, I think about (son). How he would be enjoying it or if he would like something. Every birthday, holiday, and pretty much anything we do as a family, I miss him immensely and sometimes I would just like to talk about his brief presence and how much I love that boy!

J.H.: Nobody really likes to listen to me and what happened to my little girl, they change the subject a lot. Sometimes I just keep it all in to satisfy them. I see a counselor once a week, I let it all out then

J.K.: keep telling it over and over and over again no matter how much time has passed. We are still in disbelief that our child is gone yet we wake up every day to confront that reality. Telling our stories helps with the acceptance; we all need just to function in this world.

C.B.: My sister doesn't talk about the son she lost to suicide 20 years ago but I do because I want her to know I haven't forgotten him...

L.H.T.: I found a therapist that let me do this as long and as many times as I needed to.

D.F.: Most therapists aren't helpful!! And it doesn't mean you're living in the past!! Your children are always your life no matter what!!! So if you want to talk it's okay!! I totally understand!!

W.R.F.: I talk about my son (name) it's my way of keeping him alive. I will grieve him till the day I die and no one is going to tell me different. love and miss my son (name) so much it hurts-

J.L.R: I remember telling my story, only about a month after my twins died, to someone that asked me to change the subject because I was going to make her cry. She even said "say something funny so I don't." I didn't even know how to respond to that. I just stared at her.

D.H.R.: Even husbands don't want to hear because they grieve differently

T.F.: My son was shot. I have never talked about it, not even to my therapist. I can't. Court is surely going to kill me to relive it.

T.T.: I think most people are just uncomfortable with the subject so they change the subject or all of a sudden remember something they need to do... I feel as if no one really wants to hear it ... Missing my son...

S.A.B.W.: Everyone handles death and grief differently - no right and no wrong way. Just be supportive and non-judgmental of each person's choice. I wear my heart on my sleeve - always have and always will.

G.W.: I bring (son) up a lot, it's like he's still here...and he is everywhere my heart still can't accept what my head knows is real...

It is only natural for parents to talk about their children. So why shouldn't pareavors talk about our children, even if our child is no longer alive?

There are those who are concerned that wanting to talk about our children is a sign we are not moving on and getting past the grief. The need to talk about our children doesn't usually mean we are not moving on...in fact I would say for most of us it does the opposite. It is healing to help us to process and reprocess the awful dark truth that we need to learn how to live with the permanent departure of our child from this earth.

The bottom line message to take away from this chapter? One of the best gifts you can give a pareavor is the freedom to talk about his or her child.

Words of Grace and Hope

J.O.: After almost 7 years from the loss of our (son), joy can coexist with sorrow and you can respectfully live with both! We think of (son) every day, I think of him every second of every day, but for us we can very clearly see the one set of footprints where He carried us! We are beginning to celebrate his life with love and laughter and that's good! We have missed that! I think my healing may take a lifetime; I'm a mom, but what I know is that as I walk through this journey I will embrace the joy and the tears, I will embrace the happy and the sad! I have two children, one lives in Heaven, the other lives here with me, and my heart abides with both!

C.B.: You have a choice; to allow her death to become a dropped stitch running through the tapestry of your life, or to keep her as a perfect piece in it, beautifully stitched but smaller than you wanted. Keep those 20 years as a wonderful celebration of what you had... 20 years of joy. That is what your daughter would have wanted, just as if life had played fairer and she had outlived you, you would have wanted her to do. We have to make a choice not to live in darkness, we have to allow all that we had to illuminate our lives, for they were precious times, and there will be more.

CHAPTER 5

Help! Does Anyone Else Have This Issue?

This is a chapter some of you might want to skip, but I hope not. I had to find a way to title this chapter without saying exactly what it was, because putting it as a chapter title was too morbid, and yet it is something that grieving parents deal with.

The subject is about parents who have a hard time not repeatedly seeing their child's body in their minds. This is true for almost all of us. You would think it would just be for those who either discovered their body, or those who had to view the body for identification reasons. But for most of us parents, just seeing our child lifeless, looking like they are sleeping and all we have to do is wake them up, are repeated pictures in our mind that we must deal with. If you choose to read this chapter, you will see that some parents have a much harder time getting past this than others, especially depending on the trauma of the circumstance, seeing the body of their dead child.

And there are many parents who did not see their child's body at all, but they imagine and relive what they think their child might have gone through in the death process, especially if it was a vehicle accident of some kind.

This is another topic grieving parents are quick to respond to, since we are not going to bring up to someone who has not experienced it, the difficulty of getting past seeing our child's lifeless body. In other words, it is not a subject we are "allowed" to talk about very often.

But once the question is asked, it is like a dam breaking, as it is part of the darkness we all have to deal with, and we can share it with others who fully understand. (Just a note: there were over 200 responses within 2 hours of this subject being posted on one of the grief websites.)

The following comments are a mix of grieving parents expressing their painful memories and bereaved parents helping with suggestions of how they have dealt with it.

W.P.:...I don't know how to go on. I am a medical professional, I saw him after. I know what I saw, he was gone instantly, but I keep hearing him, telling me he's hurt, I see the accident vividly, I see him trying to survive, I hear the crash. How do I make this stop? ...I know what PTSD is, I know what grief is. I've taught others, but I'm not sure how to deal with this myself.

P.L.: All I see is my son on the stretcher at the funeral home and in the casket. I was told when I see that image, immediately replace it with another, so I have a happy picture of him near where I am having the images the most; at bedtime. Also, play music. Music that has no lyrics, just instrumental. It has helped.

B.S.L.: I had to see my son dead in the ER at the same hospital where I work. ...I got a counselor that is experienced with PTSD or traumatic death...I would say things and she would say they are perfectly normal for what we've been through. Just the reassurance that I wasn't losing my mind was a huge help. I needed an anti-anxiety med to sleep at night for nearly a year...Grief is exhausting! I did yoga, I got a personal trainer, I went to my counselor, I did a grief therapy group, I did everything I could get my hands on just so I could survive.

R.L.: This is a normal part of grief. I was in the car accident and my son died. I heard, I saw, I live with it. It takes time. Get a PTSD work book and do it. It is no longer a matter of what you know. It is now a matter of what you have to do. Cry scream laugh mourn silence reach out reach in hug love weep rest. It's exhaustive and it's up to you.

D.R.R.: I was at the ER and saw my 17 yr. old daughter on the gurney all busted up… The Dr told us that she has on her license to be an organ donor. I asked God if that was the right choice. He said yes. And that is one of the ways we are able to get through the grief. Plus she gave life back to 9 people. Some of you talk about PTSD. Well I have PTSD from the Viet Nam war. And then this happened. If it were not for Compassionate friends and 1st and foremost God I would not be able to handle this. And now to top it off we lost our 31 yr old son this past Nov. It don't get any easier. But we put it all in God's hands.

L.C.: I lost my 25 yr old son with special needs, he didn't answer his phone and I raced over there to find him passed away. I can't get that vision out of my head, deceased in his bed alone, or the images of him laying in the casket at the funeral service. I can't believe he is gone, we saw each other every day and I was his caregiver…

L.M.D.: I lost my 12 year old daughter…She came into me and my husband's bedroom that morning and then just collapsed. She cried out and then went into a seizure. I immediately dialed 911. While I was on the phone with the 911 operator my husband was performing CPR on her… For a long time I was always seeing that in my head. It wouldn't go away. I kept replaying it over and over in my head. I kept seeing the doctors and nurses at the ER working on her and trying to save her. It was awful and I always cried uncontrollably when I would think about it… I still sometimes see that day in my head, but then I'll start to replace it with a happy memory of her. Or I'll also listen to music or read my Bible. It helps. This pain will always be here. I know it will truly never go away. But I do feel that time will soften the pain and maybe we won't see that image in our heads anymore. Or if we do see it, we'll know how to deal with it better and think of happy times with our child… But I'm strong in my faith in God and I know I'll see her again in heaven one day.

V.L.T.: My daughter passed away in her sleep. I am the one who found her and it has been almost three years and I think I will always recall how I found her instead of waking her up for the day, she was gone...I cannot say that finding her has ever gone away, But I recall her hugs, her smile, hearing I love you and looking at her pictures and videos and think how blessed I was to be her Mom for whatever time I had with her.

T.M.F.: My 20-yr old son had started a new medication 5 days prior he was having some side effects from, nothing serious I thought. I came home from work and found him dead, (estimated he had passed 5 hours prior). He was in a somewhat sitting position on the floor, his head slumped down...When I called 911, they suggested I start CPR...The paramedics arrived, and pronounced him dead within a few seconds. All of this happened when I was by myself 8 years ago. I had flashbacks and nightmares for many years because I didn't know how to handle or process this.

J.G.S.: I was w/ my son. I still can't get that picture out of my head. It's only 2 years but I am still there in time. It hurts so much sometimes & I wish I could have helped & done more.

C.S.J.: I went almost into auto pilot when my son arrived in the ER. I remember them showing me the CT scans and he already had a midline shift with bullet fragments in all of his brain hemispheres. The Neuro resident said something about operating and all I could do is say why would you do that he's almost brain dead. I imagine at times the image of him after being shot and thanks to my medical background, vivid TV or movies, and people making comments unknowingly I get triggered. I try to focus on how being an ICU nurse allowed me to climb in the bed with my son and hold him till he was pronounced brain dead and went for organ donation. EMDR therapy, and beginning grief therapy. Learning my triggers and trying to replace the thought. Much easier said than done. I'm only 4 months into this and now I'm struggling with he is gone more than the fact of how he went.

J.P.W.: Pray all the time and ask God to take those images from you. I know it sounds crazy right now but six years after losing my daughter I can't conjure up those images even if I try. I used to only be able to see her in the casket, in a coma, on life-

support, and having the worst seizure ever. Now at the very split second that those images start to appear... They are replaced by images of her smiling laughing, performing, and telling me she loves me.

B.P.: My daughter died of cancer, and I was holding her hand when she left. Still, the image of her on that hospital bed haunts me five years after her death...I couldn't make the image go away until it just did...

B.A.K.: For me it's been 5 1/2 years. My (2nd) daughter passed from injuries she received in a rollover crash. We sat with her for 10 days before she passed. We took her off life support on day 9. Day 10 was my youngest daughters 21st birthday. She was 31. She never woke up from the coma. ...I have good days..then a bad stretch will hit me. When I see photos of others in a hospital bed hooked up to machines it affects me. When I first saw Tim McGraw's "highway don't care" video. ...All I could do was stare and cry. The road she was on was similar...The girl so much like my daughter. She was airlifted. ..like the video. The car was the same color of her truck. I will hear a song and connect with it. It gets easier at times or as I say...it's a new normal. Keep one foot in front of the other. Find things or events to look towards. If you have other children try to focus on them...I think of my daughter every day...many times every day.

We each have certain things that trigger us back into that terrible time. For many months after my daughter died, the sound of an ambulance siren would make me freeze in fear, wondering if it was for Becca. (In her last 18 months she had a dozen ambulance rides. Several of them I either rode with her or followed behind.) One time while at the cemetery, I had a total melt-down when a medical helicopter flew over. Later I was told that it was PTS, because Becca rode in it 3 times during her last 18 months.

When it comes to the death, funeral, and burial, we are all different. Some of us do whatever it takes to stay away from things that trigger those memories (it seems men often fall in that category). Others play those memories in their minds over and over again.

The first time I saw my daughter's body I was with her husband. I had left her at the hospital a few hours earlier, but was taking the hour drive back because I felt like something wasn't right. On the way, I received the call her heart had quit, and they were not able to get it started again. So I arrived at the hospital to see her body. He had not gone in to see her yet, so we went in together (along with my other daughter who had come with me). It was so unreal, and yet I knew it was real at the same time. I actually felt like I could have spoken life back into her. My daughter told me later she thought the same thing, and one of my sons told me he felt the same way also when he saw her.

When my husband arrived, I went in with him. When my other sons went in to see her, I went in again. I didn't want to stay in there, and at the same time I wanted to go in every chance I got. Somehow, I knew it was my last chance to really see her looking like my Becca. She was peaceful, finally released from a 10 year battle, but that meant she was gone from my life for the rest of my time here on earth.

That image will always be with me. Sometimes it comes with deeper emotions than others.

As morbid as it sounds, because of the situation leading up to Becca's death, which I won't go into here but I wrote about it in my book *When Tragedy Strikes*, I took pictures of her in her casket, both opened and closed, along with other pictures on the trip to the cemetery and at the cemetery for her burial. My husband wants nothing to do with those pictures, but I looked at them often for the first year (along with the picture show we put together for her funeral).

For me, it helped me to process the fact that her spirit had left her body…that she really wasn't coming back to this earth.

As pareavors, we don't know when these memories will surface, and most of us don't know how to get rid of them. It could be years down the road when a memory hits us with a new wave of grief. If it happens when you are with us, please don't feel you have to help us think of something else to get our minds off of our child. Allow us to cry while you share a precious moment with us. We will need lots of grace, compassion, and space to grieve for the rest of our lives.

Words of Grace and Hope

C.B.: I loved my daughter above everything, but from soon after she died I was determined that she should remain a happy beacon in my memory, not an aching void in my life. I went back to work 3 months after her death, I moved forward, slowly at first, then more strongly, working through grief as it bubbled to the surface…each time it felt like a wave, fierce at first, then the waves became more gentle, then ripples. I have had a wonderfully full life with much happiness and laughter. I have had experiences I would not have had if she had lived. I would swap all of those for having had her live…but I acknowledge that life has brought me other things instead.

S.C.D.: … one must be able to separate this grief from the rest of your life. I don't forget about my son. I miss him dearly. He ended his life at the age of 21 in 2011. I found him which I am thankful for. God gave me ten more minutes with him. I was there when he took his first breath and there for his last. That, to me, was a gift. I have chosen to view many things as lessons so as not to have his death be in vain… I will always hurt and I will always cry. But I am a survivor of suicide and the grief it has brought.

CHAPTER 6

How Long Does it Take to Get Past the Darkness?

"Every now and then we wake up in the morning and feel so happy - free - complete. Those few moments of living in total bliss when our mind shields us from the pain of child loss are wonderful! And then as we get fully awake, we suddenly remember, and reality sets back in. 'My child is not here.' Our hearts sink and we want to scream out to the world, 'Why did this happen? I want my old life back when my child was with me!' The reality of child loss is the hardest part of all, because we cannot live in a world of denial. We must continue on and find our way back to life after child loss, and that is no easy thing to do" (Source unknown).

I have often asked myself, "Why am I like this? Sometimes I am just fine, and other times I am so easily agitated!" The answer? Because I am a parent who lost a child. It makes me unpredictable. I don't like being that way. It makes me feel like and come across as very unstable. But in reality, that is now part of who I am. With God's help that is changing, but I will always be capable at any moment of returning to be that fragile broken person.

When our child leaves this earth, we literally bury a part of our very flesh along with all of our hopes for the future for that child. There are people who think that at some point we should have an attitude of, "Oh well, whatever. Life goes on," and to just pick up life where it left off before the loss of our child. How absurd and ignorant! (That is putting it nicely.)

There are also way too many people who mean well, who think we should get to a point in our lives (often within a few months) where we don't fall apart; that we shouldn't continue to miss our child verbally or emotionally, and we are wrong if our continued pain causes us to be unable to function fully like we did before our child died. The things these people say and do out of ignorance can cause a lot of damage to grieving parents.

Here is a pretty good response from a pareavor to people who wrongly think this way.

> *H.W.: I have decided that people don't really care or really want to know how you feel after losing a child. But they sure want to tell you how and what you should be feeling and doing!! ... People want to tell me that I need to get over it and just move on. But how do you do that when a piece of you has been ripped away?? I don't know how to do it and I don't think that I will ever get over or be able to just move on without him!! I don't want to even if I could!! It's sad to say but I have had people delete me from Facebook and their lives. I have trouble being around large groups of people. I don't know about any of y'all but for me when I see other people with all their family with them it drives home even more that (my son) is gone and never coming back. Yes I have already been told over and over how crazy I am. But to tell the truth as of April 4, 2013 at 10:38 I did lose part of my mind and a big piece of my heart!! That's what they can't or don't want to see is part of me is gone now, and it can't or won't ever come back. So there is no way I can be the same person I was before!!*

The following are what pareavors have to say to each other about that very dark place we find ourselves in, encouraging others behind them on this path that this suffocating blackness is normal. To those who have never experienced it, this might sound depressing, but to those of us who are living it, this is confirmation which brings comfort.

H.E.L.: *I was in a severe depression for at least 5 years. I just existed...*

D.E.: *I am between year 5 and 6 after the loss of my 28 year old son, and am just coming out of the black hole...*

J.M.M.: *... I had 2 mental break downs over the last 2 years. I forgot my name, where I lived and didn't know where I was...*

J.G.: *I think it is just easier to block out the world. So you don't have to endure events and have to put on the happy face for other's who can't understand why you're not happy for them! My daughter attended a few time's with me grief counseling but made us both more angry...*

M.N.C.H.: *Grieving is not an upward scale that things will be better in time, it's more like a yo yo scale.*

Q.J.D.:. *I completely shut down for the first year. I still have days where I won't or don't want to see anyone or talk... you just give up totally because your heart feels like it will break. I have 2 daughters and 3 grandsons. Without them I wouldn't have made it...*

S.C.: *I literally went to bed for 2 years. I didn't shower, I didn't eat. I didn't talk to anyone, including my son. I wanted nothing to do with life. I had dogs and cats, friends, family, community, all willing to help, but I wanted, and still some days, want nothing to do with anyone or anything...I am 3 years, 2 months and 3 weeks out....I still can't breathe, I still fall to my knees sobbing, screaming. I do not feel with my son gone... I went to a therapist. Still do. On my own, because I knew, I would literally die, if I didn't. Most days it doesn't really help. But at least I leave the house once a week. Beginning October 1, and thru about the end of January, my level of functioning diminishes to the point of non-existent...*

R.W.: *...it's been 17 months and it's all I can do to go to a store. I go days without food because of the anxiety of going out of my house...This is the most cruel journey. Lost my mother, my brother, but it was nothing to compare to losing my child...*

D.W.H.: ... *it took me 4 years before I felt like I might want to live again.*

F.W.: *Grief comes and goes in waves, and sometimes grief triggers pop up even many years after a painful loss. I lost my son in 2001, and even to this very day I sometimes get overwhelmed with grief.*

C.R.: *...I drank myself into oblivion for 2 years (sober 7 now)...I went to a local grief support group and was the only grieving parent, the rest were widows, siblings, and adult children who lost parents. Not a good fit.*

M.H.: *... it was around 4 or 5 years before I really started to re-engage with life.*

S.C.D.: *...Unless you lose a child you cannot grasp the pain a mother is in...My brother passed away in 1986 and I was hard on my mother to shake it off. When my son died I apologized to her and told her how sorry I was because now I understand.*

E.F.M.: *I went through deep depression this year on the 20 year marker, I can tell you my other children and grands helped me through so many deep dark holes!!*

B.G.: *... I still avoid the phone. I want to spend time alone to think, try to figure out who I am now and what baby steps to take next.*

M.K.: *It's been 7yrs for me. I got on meds 2yrs ago and they help me function, that's about it. There is no fixing this; it's trying to figure out how to keep going.*

T.M.L.: *I connect on my phone (typing, not voice) with other moms who understand my pain. It's overwhelming at times (especially holidays) and to talk to people who either don't understand or want me to be/feel differently than I do drains whatever small amount of energy I have left.*

K.G.: *Death is hard but the death of a child is unspeakable. It has taken 7 yrs of anti-depressants for me to live again.*

A.J.L.: *Time is not a factor in the grieving process. Time stays still.*

W.H.: *...You come out of the fog slowly and then there are triggers which pull you back into the darkness. To the mom, her*

> *child is the only one who knows her heartbeat from the inside out...our world shattered like his windshield and our family melted that night.*
>
> *P.K.: Counselors never helped me, no one could help me but God, AND I WAS MAD AT HIM...My son died in 1989, and just the past few years, (and a new anti-depressant for PTSD) has brought me some peace. The Lord comforts me and sustains me, but it was a long time before I realized that.*
>
> *J.P.D.: I was in the deepest of holes, a place I never thought I'd get out of and never want to go back to. I adamantly said I wouldn't take medication of any kind, that's not for me, our boys and my husband didn't take meds either... It's a long rough journey we travel after the loss of a child... Nothing can "fix" this. The shock of what happens turns into the reality of what's happened and another kind of normal starts to form. None of us will ever be the same, that's just how it is...*

As you can see, many of these parents have remained in that dark, hopeless place. Some of them don't want to come out, because they are afraid it means they will start to forget their child; the pain equals not forgetting them (as if we ever could, but our minds are in so much turmoil and confusion).

Let me share with you some of the things pareavors have shared that have helped them come out of that black place.

> *L.P.: More than anything, I want people to remember my son. Don't be afraid to talk about him around me. Help me to remember the many good times that we had. He was a wonderful man who did so much for so many people when he was alive. Is it too much to ask that people remember those things and share the good times that they shared with my son, with me?*
>
> *A.E.: It will be 5 years next month since my son's death. I shut people out, even my daughter. But, she is persistent. She makes me go places with her and do things for her. I guess she*

tries to keep me occupied. It is totally aggravating, but I find myself doing whatever the task, and sometimes I even catch myself enjoying it. I never have used anti-depressants or any drug or alcohol to cover my pain. I write him letters, and go to the cemetery as often as I can. Decorate and make flower arrangements. It helps me feel like I can still have some type of relationship with him even though not physically.

J.S.: My sister-in-law would just show up and take me for a drive or we would go somewhere to eat. She found several grief groups and volunteered to go with me. She kept me moving when I wasn't capable of doing it myself... Just someone stopping by to visit for 30 minutes pulls us back into the world.

R.T.H.: To me shutting the world out is a safety mechanism, then you don't have to deal with "The Others" who don't understand and ask questions like "How many children do you have?" and "Aren't you over this yet?" etc. and you don't have to fear having a meltdown when something trips the trigger of uncontrolled crying out in public. Being out in the world makes you feel like an alien and makes you crazy that everyone else goes on with their lives like nothing ever happened...What helped me was hearing from some loving and compassionate people that they understood why I felt that way and that I could talk about my son with them openly and freely, and someone told me that "I" was the one to carry my son's legacy and let his light still shine for the world to see, or I could keep him stuck within my four walls with me, I was asked what I would want him to be doing if it was me who left instead of him, and that he would be much more proud of me if I lived for him and I both.

C.M.: Visit her as often as you can....say her son's name and reminisce about happy, funny stories....let her cry, just hug her and tell her you love her......if it takes her forever to come to her new normal, let her heal in her own time and own way. She may never quite be her old self, but she can become more integrated into a new world without him....let her cry...hold her hand...call her on his birthday and on the day he died........order her a memory fleece blanket from Living Social or a calendar of his photos at Staples. Help her celebrate his life even though he *isn't here. We want our children to live on in memory, heart, soul and mind. Knowing he isn't forgotten is soooo important.*

There is hope. We *can* come out of our darkness and live again. We *can* have a productive life, enjoying the time we have left here on earth with our loved ones and friends. We *can* choose to be a victor in our tragic circumstances instead of remaining a victim. And we need to have those around us who will be there for us with love and grace as we work through the process.

Words of Grace and Hope

C.D.: After my daughter died at 10 years old, six years ago, it would have been easier to die than it was to face the idea of living without her. But one night I was out walking with my husband and I realized that I know she is in heaven and I'll be there with her one day for ETERNITY. Who knows how much longer I would have on the earth with my living children? I knew then that I needed to make the hard choice of joining the living again for the sake of my living children and grandchildren whom all needed me. And not only living, but trying to find some way to actually get some good out of the life I had left.

E.B.A.: Someone said to me, upon the death of my son, "It never gets better. It only gets worse." Not true! That is a choice! I will say the first many years are just bad. But there is and will be joy. And there will come a time, when there is more joy, than there is sorrow. I CHOOSE to be joyful. Life does go on, and there are many reasons to be joyful…

CHAPTER 7

| | | | | | |

Does Losing a Child Have Any Physical Effects?

I did not know until a year and a half after Becca's death that a person can literally have a broken heart. It affects the left ventricle, even changing the shape of the heart, as part of the heart temporarily enlarges and doesn't pump well, while the rest of the heart functions normally or with even more forceful contractions. And as a note, based on the research I have done, it happens almost exclusively with women. It causes heart attack–like symptoms, and is called broken heart syndrome, stress-induced cardiomyopathy or takotsubo cardiomyopathy (based on its official discovery in Japan). Other names for it are transient apical ballooning syndrome, apical ballooning cardiomyopathy, and, Gebrochenes-Herz-Syndrome. With all of those names, how did I not know it existed?

For someone who has lost a child, the stress does not go away for months and years, which means it can be an ongoing condition. The good news is that if this is the case, it can be controlled by medication. Since this involves the heart, it is important to get checked by a doctor if these heart-attack symptoms are happening.

So what else happens to us physically? You name it, and we deal with it, often opposite things at the same time. Our minds are confused, our emotions are in shambles, and our bodies don't know where to get their directions from.

Here is something I read, with no name attached to it.

Inability to focus. Overeating. Undereating. Sleeping too much. Never able to sleep. Panic attacks. Fear. Insecurity. Anxiety. Inability to trust life. Outbursts of tears. Waves of crazy emotions. This is only a partial list of what happens to a parent when child loss occurs.

How did parents respond to this list of issues?

B.S.M.: I have all these symptoms. It's been six months for me, seems to be getting worse

K.D.G.: It's been a year and I still can't focus on anything. I had PTSD and it was crippling. Finally got rid of that and now just sad and numb.

F.S.B.: Almost 3 years, and describes it all.

C.M.: Sometimes we worry - really worry a lot - that since our child died we're going crazy. We forget things easily. We are like robots in our daily routine. We repeat ourselves when talking. When driving we get afraid that we're lost -- we can't remember where we're going. We wander -can't complete a task as simple as peeling an orange. We cry and then we turn to rage. In simple terms, we're a mess!!!! If only someone would explain to us at the very beginning of this journey of loss that all of these things are typical of a person going through deep, heartbreaking grief. This won't last forever (thank goodness!), but it's scary when it's happening and most people don't want to talk about it. Why? We're afraid we'll get committed to the hospital. We're afraid we'll lose our jobs. We're afraid people will shun us. We're just afraid of everything.

K.T.: It's just a lil over 2 years and I still feel like this. It's so hard for others to understand how u feel and why you act like you do.

L.M.G.: this is all so true, and it takes years, not months to feel better.

L.D.W.: 2 years 2 months for me and I still experience all of these. 8 months ago I went to the emergency room because I could not stop crying. I am now on meds for depression/anxiety and feel a little better but it still comes in waves.

K.J.: 6 years later I feel this way at times. No one seems to understand, not even those in the medical profession. One doctor confused these feelings with the symptoms of ADD; especially the lack of focus and inability to sleep.

L.A.B.M.: My son passed almost a year now and it feels like yesterday. I used to be able to remember everything. I was organized. Now I can't sleep. Cry over everything. And the emotional outbursts are terrible. I over eat and under eat. The biggest thing is I miss him so bad. So do his 3 children...

T.T.: U mean everyone does this?? I thought was just me and I had dementia or sumthin ... Has been a little over 2 years and I still run on autopilot most days; gets better, then back to square one and the pain is so very real...

L.M.H.: I know this feeling all too well. October is ALWAYS a VERY HARD month for me. My (son) would be 21 years old. I often wonder what kind of young man he would be.

C.W.N.: This is so my life... And it still is over five years later

J.H.: I agree....to anyone that thinks 'you can get over it' has never lost a child. The chronic pain lasts the rest of your life here on earth. The hurt is REAL and DEEP.

K.J.: people just don't know that medically there is such a thing as a broken heart and this happens to people who lose a child. Diagnosed 3 years ago with broken heart by a doctor and I think I will die with it. miss my baby... 6 years old died of brain tumor. And no one will talk about your baby that died although my family loved her too

L.K.: It's been 2 years for me and people say I need to move on; that's what she'd want. Hmm news flash, I know what she'd want. I don't need u pointing it out for me. It's like they think I like feeling this way. I didn't ask for this...I'm living my own worst nightmare.

L.K.D.: Two years and it still happens, changed only in that I have learned to live with it.

K.J.: So so so true. I can't remember people's names and it's so embarrassing but I tell them sometimes I can't remember my own name. So not funny...

D.R.: *It's pure torture*
P.G.F.: *This is me and I did lose my job of 23 years*
B.O.: *It has been almost 8 years since I lost my 16 yr old son and I still have these moments.*
L.U.B.: *I don't think anyone can imagine all of the suffering that goes with this if they haven't been through it.*
L.S.: *All this stuff is normal and eventually settles down. I can't tell u how comforting it was to know that when I was going thru it...*
L.S.M.: *I keep thinking that I have dementia...good to know.*
S.J.H.: *I feel exactly like that! I try to explain it to people and they just shrug me off.*
S.P.D.: *It's been over a year and I'm still convinced I am going to end up in a rubber room. So many have given up on us because we don't follow through with invitations, answer every phone call and text. Those who truly love us understand we are not the same but we are trying.*

  I can't tell you how many times I am driving down the street and suddenly panic because I totally forgot where I am going, or I forgot how to get to somewhere I have driven to dozens of times before and don't know where to turn. There are times I walk out of a store, and have absolutely no idea where my car is. I admit I am a bit scatter-brained by nature and used to do this on occasion before Becca was gone. But this is different. It is like there is no information in the brain to pull on. Everything is blocked, and I freeze in a panic because I don't even have the thoughts to know where to start looking. I have actually wandered around a parking lot with a cart, fighting tears, trying to get my bearings as to where my car is. It's one thing to forget something and laugh at yourself for your forgetfulness. It is completely different when it comes with panic and feeling like you are losing your mind because your thoughts are so jumbled.
  Things like this make us start wondering if early Alzheimer's is setting in, and it is scary and unnerving!

If you know someone who has lost a child, please be gentle with them in the area of their health, including their mental health. We already know there are times we aren't taking very good care of ourselves. That's because of how often we are in survival mode. When we are ready, you will hear us start talking about needing to become more disciplined in our lives in certain areas. At that point, tread lightly, and ask if there is any way you can help us with it.

Words of Grace and Hope

A.B.Y.W.: My daughter has been gone for almost 8 years... I remember the first days I was in a fog ... didn't eat, didn't sleep much, and just kinda like a zombie...It is hard .. I know the first time I laughed I felt too guilty ...and yet it felt good to laugh... Just take it one day at a time, no, one hour at a time, no, sometimes you have to take it one min at a time ... I always say it is like I have a thin scab on my heart and every once in a while the scab gets pulled off and here I go again .... but it heals a little again and I get on down the road... You try and take care of you as best as you can... I now am thankful to God for the time I did have with her...32 years ... She was my gift from God ...

R.W.: My daughter has been gone for 9 years. I do think of her every day, but I have very little doom and gloom. I can remember early on that I thought I would never laugh or have a good time again. We started watching Funniest Videos in order to start laughing. I went to family parties and tried to enjoy myself. It took a while. Wish I could tell you when I began to feel more normal but it was a gradual thing. I joined a fitness club and socialized with friends. I went into counselling for a year so I would not get "stuck." I enjoy my family now, go on cruises, and develop new interests and friends. I am lighthearted most of the time. Do I wish I had my daughter back? Absolutely! But there is still a lot to look forward to.

CHAPTER 8

How Do I Deal With My Child's Birthday?

We try to prepare ourselves for the two days that are often the hardest two days of the year; our child's birthday and anniversary of their death. But it seems quite often we still are not prepared for the full range of emotions that can sweep over us on those days.

I was recently surprised to learn that my husband has a third date that is just as difficult for him. It is the date on which he adopted Becca…the day the legal papers were signed that acknowledged she was his daughter, and he was her daddy. So for those parents who lost a child who was adopted, it goes beyond just the birthday. There is a day they silently grieve to themselves, because so few people understand, even us pareavors. So even though this chapter is about how we deal with the birthday of our child who is no longer with us, I wanted to take a moment to acknowledge that "extra" day most of us don't have to deal with, and say I am sorry for your loss that goes just as deep as the rest of us. I am so very sorry that you have to go through a third day that the rest of us do not have.

For all of us, it can be so very difficult to think about, much less celebrate, the birth of our child who is no longer with us. Some of us can get to the point where we can celebrate the blessing of the time we had with our child, and some cannot.

Many parents find they can be okay for a couple of years, and then for some reason the birthday hits us hard once again, leaving us a wreck.

> *Anonymous: I've gone through all the classes and certifications to help others on their journey after the death of a child, but I have yet to cross this bridge myself. My daughter would have turned 16 on February 1st of this year. Every year I go through the same motions. She died at 5 after being sedated for a broken wrist and never regaining consciousness. I usually try to get together with friends and family for her birthday so that I'm not alone. But no matter how many people are around I still feel alone in a room filled with people.*

Far too many people question why we still want to find a way to acknowledge our child's birthday when they are no longer here. It is because we gave birth to a human being. That is a big deal! And just because he or she is no longer on this earth, it does not erase that fact or the memory of that day, nor does it take away our instantly fierce and intense love for that little bundle of joy that came into our lives that day.

Here are some parents sharing with each other the things they have done (or are doing) to help them ease the pain of the yearly birthday. You will see there are so many precious ways to honor and remember the day our child came into this world.

> *M.C.M.:…This year, I wished I was making him a birthday cake instead of missing him and feeling sad. So I made that cake and took it to the local men's homeless shelter. I think that will become my new tradition.*
> *L.F.K.: I have a picnic at the cemetery and take (son) a balloon bouquet!*
> *D.B.C.: We just lost our 13 year old daughter. I am going to celebrate her life and have cake. Then we are going to release 13 balloons with messages of what we loved about her. I'm sure there will be tears, but we can share the good memories she gave us too.*
> *K.C.: We go out and we pick a different place every year. We also order a dessert and ask that they put a candle in it for us.*

How Do I Deal With My Child's Birthday?

L.P.P.: I go out and buy special cuddle animals and take them to the children at the Children's Advocacy Center in my daughter's name. Reaching out to other children eases the pain for me.

T.A.R.: Each year on my angel son's birthday we cook a complete meal for 100 homeless individuals. It is his birthday party and I believe it makes him very happy to be remembered on his birth date by helping others.

E.H.:... no matter what we do it is still a void. I hate the birthday worse than the anniversary of his death! That was the day all the future was planned and then taken away. I always do something by myself and then in his memory I take two filled back packs to the school to some child who needs it and always include the party money and a nice surprise for the child getting it. The only requirement is no one is ever to know where they come from but the school counselor. It seems to help me get through the day...This tradition has been going on since 1987.

J.W.T.: My son's birthday is December 9 so we do a big toy drive or get a list from our children's hospital and gather the things they need donated and take it up there. This year over 4000 dollars' worth of clothes, gift cards, and toiletries were donated in (son's) name... It's our way of allowing him to live on through good deeds

T.T.C.: I have a birthday party every year. (Daughter) loved celebrating her birthday and having everyone around her help blow out the relight candles. So I have a party with everything she liked, decorating cookies, swimming, bounce house

T.J.M.J.:...The first few years I bought the types of gifts I normally would give him and donated them to charities in his name.

R.O.: We celebrate (daughter's) birthday with her sister and her family. Others aren't included because it's just too hard to deal with their discomfort. I make a donation to (daughter's) scholarship fund and a mini loan to someone I know she would support. It's always hard, but we do our best. It's been ten years.

C.L.W.: ...Our family always celebrates my son's birthday by having his favorite meal. We have his favorite cake too and we share memories about him, usually funny ones because laughter is truly the best medicine.

M.D.: it is really hard. My friends are having sweet 16 parties for their children & I feel like there's a knife being plunged in my heart because I don't get to celebrate her sweet 16 & they expect me to be in a celebratory mood for their children.

L.P.: My daughter...loved birthdays and loved celebrating - so that's what we have done each year. We loved going to Dodger games, so, friends & family attend a Dodger game in her honor -80-100 of us...

L.L.: I lost my oldest daughter when she was almost 16, in 1985. Even though it's been such a long time ago, some years are still harder than others. Three of my other daughters and I try to plan a get together on or near her birthday. We go out to eat and I take her photo album, baby book or whatever we want. We light a candle for the table and just talk about her and share memories.

C.N.: I write a letter saying all I can think of, then burn it and let the smoke carry it on.

G.W.: We meet at the cemetery with family and friends and release balloons for our son's birthday. Even others that cannot be there have said they released balloons from their home at the same time we do. We then eat some brownies or cupcakes. It's just not the same as a bday party but I will forever be there to release balloons for him.

D.E.P.: We go out for dinner at the same restaurant we took her to on her last birthday on earth. We tell our favorite (daughter) stories and drink a toast to her.

A.S.: I always make a pink cake with pink frosting. I celebrate to myself. I remind myself of how my daughter impacted others through her life and death. I used to celebrate with others, however, I found that even among others I feel alone. I realized I could better console myself.

P.K.: Last year I bought myself & him tulips. My mom brought me the most beautiful tulips to the hospital the day he was born.

D.P.C.: I spend my morning crying. When I can't cry any longer I pull myself together, have lunch with hubby and we usually buy something (like a plant) in their memory. They would be 6 in April.

R.L.: We held a bowling fundraiser and the funds went to the science department at the high school.

A.B.S.: We serve a meal at the Ronald McDonald House that we stayed at during our daughter's illness and death...

C.J.: We celebrate our daughter's birthday. She left two kids so they get to blow out the candles.

L.S.M.: I bought myself earrings with his birthstone on them and I put them on and have worn them ever since. Also we spent the time camping because he loved that.

U.G.U.B.: My daughter who died at the age of 17 loved macaroni and cheese and Carmel Frappuccinos. So her friends and I started a celebration each year on her birthday to eat those. It's been a tradition for the past 8 years and I don't see it ever stopping. It helps me celebrate her life rather than mourn the loss.

D.A.B.: I just lost my son in December... I quit my job. I can't make myself go out of the house. I don't want to talk to anyone including my remaining kids. All I do is cry...I had a friend who wrote me a letter & told me that she now goes crazy decorating for Christmas in honor of her granddaughter. That struck me - instead of avoiding happy occasions, use them as opportunities to celebrate & honor the life of the one who is gone. I can hardly wait for next Christmas to show my son how much I love him.

We're certain of one thing - we want our child with us, but we know that's not possible. And that is the part that breaks our heart over and over again. But as the last parent discovered, we can either choose to continue to mourn their death, or we can celebrate and honor their life.

Maybe you can suggest helping a pareavor do one of these ideas to help them celebrate and honor their child. Even if they say no, you can be sure they will be touched that you thought of them and acknowledged their child's special day.

Words of Grace and Hope

L.W.: I write in a journal, to (son), my 29 yr old son, who was the victim of a hit and run car crash. I also go on a long walk, by myself, at the beach, in a park or just around the neighborhood, and acknowledge the Sovereignty, Majesty and power of God. God gave me my son for 29 years. Now, he is at his permanent home, in Heaven, and I'll join him there in God's timing. I also buy a small gift for my 2 grandchildren, in honor of their Uncle's b-day. We talk about him and how much he loved them, and that they will see him again in Heaven.

N.P.C.: We can't control what happened, but we can control how we choose to look at it. We were blessed to have them even though time was cut short. We still need to have gratitude for the remaining beautiful things in our lives. Moments or days of sadness will happen, but so should moments of joy and laughter.

CHAPTER 9

||||||

What About the Dreaded Anniversary Date?

Getting to the point where we can actually celebrate the day our child came into the world is very possible. But their departure date is a whole different event. And it goes far beyond just that day. There are so very many memories we wish we did not have, and want to erase from our lives.

- The last time we saw or spoke to them
- Where we were when we received the news, or worse, when we found their body
- The first person we had to tell
- Going to the funeral home to make arrangements, including picking out a coffin or an urn
- Choosing a cemetery plot for our child
- Putting together picture boards and slide shows of their life that would never be added to
- The memorial service and/or funeral
- The clothes we wore to those services (will we ever wear them again?)
- The drive to the cemetery and the service there
- Trying to write thank-you cards (unless someone graciously did it for us)
- Our first visit to the gravesite alone
- The first time we fully realized our child would never walk inside our door again
- The first time we sobbed in agony in their room or holding something that belonged to them

- And on and on it goes…

Many parents dread the entire month, and can fall apart to the point where they are unable to function year after year. It can be such a heavy, heavy time in our lives. Here is what one mom had to say coming up on the first year anniversary.

> *J.H.: The first anniversary of my son's death is coming up on the 15th. I think this is almost worse than when he died last year. It's like I know he will be dead in 12 days. This is killing me. I'm so depressed. I wish I could just sleep the month away.*

These parents are discussing with each other how they get through the most horrific time of their lives each year, tenderly giving suggestions to others who are newly facing this painful trauma.

> *M.S.: For the first year I just was very gentle on myself, no fanfare no expectation. Much crying of course. Some people came over for comfort. When the day comes, the most important thing is to do what's best for you.*
> *N.C.: From my experience the days leading up to the actual day will most likely be the hardest. Do what you need to do to get through that day. Everyone is different, some like to be alone and others like to be with family & friends. I went to the cemetery for a while and spent the rest of the day with family. Go easy on yourself.*
> *D.C.I.: It'll be 7 years next month for me, and, I still dread the month of April. We send up balloons, and decorate her grave.*
> *T.L.L.:…on his Angelversary… I just go sit with him and talk with him….I can't celebrate the day he "went home"….*
> *Q.S.C.: The days leading up to it will be worse than the actual day, the dread and grief is gut wrenching… On the one-year anniversary, my daughters and I decided to have a celebration of*

his life for family, neighbors and his high school friends. It kept my mind busy with planning and brought me a sense of calm knowing that he wouldn't be forgotten. We did a balloon release and lit votive candles that spelled out his name as the sun went down. It was a beautiful evening. Everyone is different though, so just follow your heart and do what gives you peace.

K.L.: The best way to handle the anniversary is to do what would make you the most comfortable. If that means staying in bed eating ice cream all day, so be it (just don't make it a habit). We went to (son's) favorite beach on his first anniversary and flew kites and went boogie boarding (his favorite things at the beach), then went to one of his favorite restaurants for lasagna.

D.V.K.:...for 5 years we send up 24 yellow balloons with messages to my son. Age 24, favorite color yellow...certain people join us and each year some new people come...we feel better although emotional...after, we go to have coffee and cake , sort of a tradition of the Greek memorial service...

K.A.:....I change my calendar every month 2 days before the 29 so I never hit the date.

S.Q.G.: I was a hot mess in the 2-3 weeks leading up to the first anniversary. ...I felt like my son was going to die all over again. It was awful but there's no way to skip over those calendar dates. Just be around supportive fam and friends and don't make any rules on how to handle things. Be flexible, be open; if you want to spend the actual day in bed crying, do that. If you want to create a memorial event do that. However you get through it, know that we have been there and understand.

T.S.O.: I started to go on vacation. She left a little boy behind, my grandson... at 8 yrs old I have noticed he looks down on these dates so I decided we will take him on vacation to his happy place (Disney world). This past Nov we went, and it made a big difference in our lives. He was happy and it made me happy to see him happy.

J.B.: It was 3 years ago that I lost my (son) aged 22. He died in a motorbike accident. The first year I drove the 180 miles to be where it happened. Last year I wasn't strong enough to stand where my boy took his last breath. This year I felt I had to be there. Every year, every day we feel different.

D.A.: The first couple of years were the hardest for me. The "firsts," then the "never agains," then the new things we try because the old has too much pain. I'm now on my year 17 and it's still hard but it's just all different.

M.B.: Each Monday I wear pink in my daughter's honor. On the 13th of each month, I wear black for mourning. I schedule a day off on the death anniversary and one on her birthday and I reserve these days as my own to grieve as I need.

D.C.D.: it's been 17 yrs for us. The first yr was such a blur I'm not sure what we did. Now we light a memory candle. We often go to one of her favorite places. I've learned having a plan helps and the anticipation is much worse than the actual day.

P.E.: My son will be gone 9 years in December; every anniversary I light a candle; all holidays I decorate his grave. I also do a lot of fundraising like walks, or bowling which helps. I find it comforting; it doesn't bring him back, but helping others is what he liked to do. It's very hard

R.C.: I dreaded the first anniversary of my 18 year old daughter's death. I took 19 balloons to her grave site and planted a lilac bush in my backyard, took the day off from work and tried to think of all the good times…

P.R.:…writing him a letter seems to help me any time there is an anniversary or just a time when missing him becomes unbearable.

S.M.:…His "trademark" to bring a box of glazed donuts to the house…I'm asking family members to enjoy a "greasy donut" that day in his memory. Also planning to spend the day with my daughter and work a bit in the garden, which I'm putting together in his memory.

S.P.: When the first anniversary came we went to her favorite place, the beach, and we brought flowers to let go in the ocean in her memory…

L.O.: What helped me get through the day was taking it easy upon myself and doing something to honor him and my relationship with him. We went to graveside, we flew a sky

> *lantern from his grave, we made his favorite food for dinner......*
> *Everyone is different, but the theme of rituals runs through these comments here. I think rituals play an important part in healing... Thinking about "honoring" as well as grieving helps me.*

As you can see, it isn't just the anniversary day of the death. It is the days (and sometimes weeks) leading up to it that cause dread and grief for many of us. Every year we have to once again face the unnatural and painful fact that our child departed from this earth before we did.

And as you can also see, it is a very personal and individual yearly event. Many of us isolate ourselves or spend it with a very small group (a spouse and/or our other children). Personally, my family doesn't seem to want to acknowledge this dark day in our lives. However, this year on the 4th anniversary of Becca's death, I am having a "launch party." It is the day I have chosen to put this book in your hands out in the market for sale.

We need prayer, love, and lots of space.

Words of Grace and Hope

> *J.M.C.: I held a "Happy Heavenly Birthday" party for my son on the first birthday after his passing. It helped all of us to make it through the day and remember the happy times with him, telling stories, laughing, loving, and crying at times throughout the day, but I made it through the day feeling good about it, and knowing that nobody forgot him.*
>
> *D.A.: My oldest son went to heaven 5 years ago. That first year I felt so much sadness and gloom. I thought life would end. But then I put my faith and trust in a loving God. At first feeling like He was not loving, or why would he let my son die? But God did not let him die, He gave him a life more abundant than life here would ever give him. I learned to laugh and smile and live again. I miss my son every day and some days are still hard, but I live in joy again, because I know whom I believe, and will one day see him again. I love to read in the psalms.*

David who wrote most of the book lived in grief and joy and hope, and poured his heart out to God, and God heard him and delivered him. He will for you too.

CHAPTER 10

Why Can't People Understand That I Can't Quit Missing My Child?

     I don't know of many moms who had the blessing of giving birth to a child, and then losing that child at some point through death, who does not keep a picture of that child in her wallet. My picture of Becca is front and center, so that every time I snap it open I see her smiling at me. You would think this would be a painful thing, and it is, but it is also a comfort in feeling like my child is always with me, will always be a part of me, and will never be forgotten.

     Many of us, especially mothers, also have an extra something we wear (which includes getting a tattoo). Oftentimes no one else even knows about it. We don't advertise it, we don't call attention to it; it's just always there with us.

     A few months after Becca died, we went on vacation to Branson, Missouri. I grew up in Joplin, and loved going to Silver Dollar City. I introduced my own family to this place, and now Dave and the kids enjoy returning there as much as I did growing up. On this particular trip, as we were wandering in and out of the shops, there was one that really got my attention. They engraved band rings. It was within the first year of losing Becca, and something about it gripped me, causing me to want a ring with her name on it. I wear it on my right pinky. On the left side of her name is engraved a little heart, and on the right side of her name is engraved a small butterfly. Why is something like that so important to us? I don't really know. It just is. Somehow it keeps them close to us, even though they are now so very far away.

Sometimes when we say, "I still miss my child so much!" people respond with, "Yes, I miss her, too." Other times people give us a strange look. Then there are those who let us know they think it is time to move on and get past it.

In today's world, it is so easy to see and interact with our offspring. Even with adult children who have moved away, there are ways to see them occasionally. You can pretty much call them whenever you want, and still plan parties, vacations, and other family events together. Most parents haven't thought about the fact that they would almost have to make a conscious decision *not* to have access to their child! If they were to just stop and think for a moment what life would be like without their child for a full month, with absolutely no contact whatsoever, how would they feel? Now take that thought and make it for the rest of their lives here on earth. Just maybe, society would view the grief from child loss a little differently. Child loss is an empty ache that never goes away - ever. Child loss is in a category of pain and heartache that is different from any other loss.

I read in a book about a woman who told a grieving mom she knew how she felt, because her daughter was moving out of the country. Of course this woman stayed in contact with her daughter, even though she was across the world, and several years later, she made a trip to go visit her grandchildren...something the pareavor would never be able to experience. You tell me, is it the same? Doesn't this bereaved mom have the right to still miss her child, and occasionally grieve deeply for other losses in her life that resulted in the death of her daughter?

Some parents become either withdrawn, or angry and bitter when they are given limits by people around them on missing their children. When others question our grief, at the very least, we have to struggle to keep it from adding to our heaviness. But don't just take my word for it. Here are what some pareavors have to say about those who don't seem to

Why Can't People Understand That I Can't Quit Missing My Child?

even try to understand the suffocating darkness we find ourselves in.

> *M.C.: No one could possibly be prepared for the devastation of child loss. No one can understand this terrible journey we are on unless they are experiencing the same journey. When someone doesn't seem to understand that I am now a different person since we lost our precious daughter, I calmly say "I sincerely hope you never understand."*
>
> *J.W.H.: I'd never wish this on anyone just so they'd know how we feel, but it does add to the hurt that people as a whole seem to think that it's something you just get over, forget & move on! That is so not true! We learn to cope (although I don't always do it well on many days) & yes, life goes on & we can even enjoy many things, but our loss is still always there, sometimes in the background, yet often in the forefront. We can burst into tears anytime, anywhere & when that happens it's just as raw as if it happened that day! ...All I know is that unless you have experienced it you really don't know what it feels like day after day, so please don't expect those of us who have, to act like our loss is trivial!*
>
> *L.D.: I can remember, in the first month after (daughter) left, demanding that God give her back, and believing she would suddenly appear.......... Our minds just cannot accept that our most loved and precious, irreplaceable child, all grown up and living their own life, fulfilling their life long hopes and dreams, has died. Never to be able to hug them again, smell their hair, have those hour long phone calls every day, about any and everything, that always left you with a smile on your face, or shaking your head, knowing she'd have to figure this one out for herself. It is impossible to erase 33 years of falling head over heels in love with them, all over again, every single day of their life. Impossible for our eyes to accept they can't find them, when it seems like they were just there. That physical longing to touch them, an overwhelming need that drives you to your breaking point. It's so very hard to imagine living a life like this. It's even*

a million times harder when you find yourself actually living this nightmare, that we are to now call our life! May God hold all of us closely in his arms today, while we struggle to accept that which we cannot change!

S.B.: I have often wished my "lost" friends could understand for just 1 minute the feeling of never seeing or talking to their child (not wishing that they lose their child just that they feel) then maybe they would know how we feel every minute of every day.

E.P.: We lost our daughter 15 years ago and now our eldest grandson was killed on Saturday 24th. So unfair. My son is now going through what we went through all those years ago. The pain in his eyes is horrible to see. To be able to turn back time or stop time would be the best gift in the world.

L.D.: In order to try a day in my shoes, a friend of mine decided to imagine that her daughter wasn't on this earth for a day............she couldn't even get out of bed because the very thought of it devastated her. Then she realized that she could stop her nightmare but mine would continue.

L.L.P: Yep the worst pain in the world.....someone could shoot me and the pain would be more bearable than the pain I feel every day

K.G.C.: I would never wish this pain and heartache on anyone. Almost 18 years without my beautiful daughter and it is still as fresh as the day it happened. I still want to talk and laugh with her. Wonder who you would be now...

J.H.: I have given up trying to explain to people how it is different from any other loss. I have just had my daughter's 7th anniversary; I also lost my husband, both to cancer. I had someone who I thought was a friend, post a comment in reply to something I had posted on a grief page on how she didn't realize how my grief was still so painful, as if I should be over it by now.

K.S.: My wonderful son died 13 months ago in a horrific head-on collision. Tomorrow, I will attend my niece's baby shower and I am terrified of crying at her party. I do not want to take any joy out of her special day...Unfortunately, people are not tolerating my agony. Because of this, I rarely attend get-

Why Can't People Understand That I Can't Quit Missing My Child?

togethers...I REALLY do not want to go but my elderly aunt is counting on me for a ride.

J.S.: I have had to explain my absence from weddings of my daughter's friends. It is just unbearable that I will never see her daddy walk her down an aisle.

B.H.H.: As we all know, common sense is not common. Sometimes people can be so insensitive, it has been 2 months and 12 days since we lost our only child, the other day someone said to me "well I guess you are used to not seeing or talking to her by now, right?". I could have cheerfully stabbed them in the heart, as they had just done to me.

A.A.: Losing a child is a life sentence! I have cried every day for the last 2 years since losing my son who was only 22...unless they have been through it themselves they can never understand the pain of losing a child ever! It destroys you as a person to be honest!

M.H.: people can be cruel and senseless... losing a child is a pain like no other... it never goes away nor does time heal, as it lives with us forever

J.H.: If only I could go back 2 normal everyday problems; problems that can be solved or just don't matter. Child loss is forever. Child loss can nearly kill you with the pain. You learn to live with it but your life is ruined forever.

E.A.: After my son died, my closest friend who was very religious kept telling me "All is well." I know she meant well, but every time she said that I wanted to scream. All was NOT well, my son had died!

Just a few days ago, while working on this book, I was accused by someone of trying to drag up the past instead of going forward. Wow! My response? "If you were to ever lose one of your children from this earth, you would come to find out that the death of a child (no matter what their age) takes you to a very dark place of grief, for a very long time. We want to help other parents who find themselves in this horrible place to find hope and life again, beyond that death.

For Dave and me, *it isn't bringing up the past; it is learning how to live in the present and in the future without our daughter*, which is the same thing as every other parent who has to deal with, how wrong it is to bury your child."

As bereaved parents, we will never stop missing our child. It is impossible, because they are a part of our very being. They are a lost link to our everyday lives, and to our future. Please don't expect us to, or be surprised by it.

Words of Grace and Hope

S.W.: The movie Tangled always gets me.... the ending when she sees her parents after all those years.... just thinking about it brings me to tears. Oh how glorious will that day be. I KNOW in my heart that there is a heaven and that we will see our dear children again. I can't wait for the day that I will see my son again... but until that day... I live for my family here and find joy in them...

S.W.: ... Knowing God has helped me...This morning I am not crying as I am peacefully thinking of my son who died (three years ago today). It does not mean that something won't trigger tears later in the day, but I talked with my sister on the phone this morning and we laughed and chatted...This is called grief, and as loving, caring parents we must suffer this because of the loss of our child that we loved so dearly... Your child will always be with you, in your heart, in your memories and in your soul...

CHAPTER 11

||||||||||

What About Melt Downs and Grief Attacks?

You probably don't see us have these moments, and therefore be surprised by what you read here. (Remember how good we are at putting on our masks?)

Melt downs actually happen frequently, daily for many parents, especially in the first one to three years or so.

Grief attacks happen out of the blue for the rest of our lives.

As an interesting note, I found more dads vocalizing about this issue than any other.

> *M.S.: It doesn't have to be a Mom, I'm a Dad and I cried at least once a day for four hundred straight days. Now after three years I may be fine for days, then all of a sudden, here it comes…it knows no gender.*
> *M.H.: My daughter has been gone almost 13 years, my son 8 months tomorrow, it took me two years to come out of the fog after she passed, now there is not a day goes by I am not on my knees in a complete melt down! I know it is going to take time, and just lean on God!*
> *D.H.M.: Life becomes a roller coaster.*
> *A.E.W.: My son passed away 4 yrs ago on Mar. 29. There is not a day that goes by that I don't think of him. Some days it's instant tears and others a smile comes to my face thinking about him. At first there were tears every day and more than once a day. As a mother, I don't think you ever truly get over it. You just learn to live around it.*

L.J.D.: *I lost my son 25 years ago. There are still days that it feels like just yesterday that we buried him. I still…wander through the house looking for him before I wake up enough to realize it was just a dream… I didn't think I would make it a week and now it has been 25 years. The emotions lessen as time goes on but they never go away. That is OK though, because the worst would be to not remember them!*

L.F.E.: *I lost my son in 2010. I can hold it together but an unexpected trigger will bring me to tears. If I speak to one of his former friends, that could break my composure. Or walking into his bedroom. Or hearing one of his favorite songs. The list goes on and on.*

H.M.: *I recently had one of these attacks. It's been almost five years since my only child died and this one hit hard. I kept saying, "I thought I was doing better," but I have to remember….there is no "better."*

L.P.S.: *so many times I was in the middle of shopping and I just left my shopping cart with frozen food in the middle of the store and fled because I lost it out of the blue. It took a while, and it slowed down gradually. It gets better. IT GETS BETTER. It never goes away, but it gets better.*

P.B.: *I'm 5.5 years since the loss of (son). I still have these attacks. However, sometimes I will now have an attack of smiling and joy at the memories. In the beginning, I remember saying ALL THE TIME, "Every memory is a reminder he is gone." Sometimes this is still very true and I am a puddle on the floor. But, oh! Those precious times of joy!*

M.C.: *I finally figured out that these attacks are never going away. I just wish I had some warning……*

P.L.G.: *I have withdrawn from so much because of this. I try and fail to be what others think I should be and it hurts.*

P.B.: *My friend told me these moments are proof they did exist. I agree. When you lose a child who has left no children, it does feel sometimes like, was he real? The pain is real. The memories are real. Proof he did exist. My son was 25. It has been 15 years. My only child. I miss him and I miss me.*

M.C.: My (daughter) is gone 28 years. At Christmas in the car with my granddaughter I heard the theme from the Karate Kid and I just sobbed. My lovely 20 year old said: Grammer, now I understand. It is never gone, it just comes less often, but just as intensely.

G.R.: (As a father) it's been over 25 years since I lost my daughter, and although life is mostly normal, every once in a while, a particular song, or smell, or situation will bring the emptiness back to full, heartbreaking, force.

W.G.T.: I lost my son 16 yrs ago and I still have moments that I just sit down and cry.

L.W.G.: After 12 years, I still cry at the oddest moments. It's a testament of the love between a parent and child. One day I figured out how many days it had been since I hugged my girl. It was over 4,000, and I cried off and on all day…

P.M.H.M.: It has been 8 years for me since I lost my daughter at 17 and a song or smell can still bring me to my knees.

S.L.: My (son) died 4 years ago at the age of 39. Some days I am ok and can enjoy time spent with friends and family. Then, without warning, I still have huge emotional crashes. I have had to leave stores more times than I can remember when I would see moms with their grown sons shopping, laughing, arguing, teasing each other. I have broken down at the reminder that I will never have those experiences again.

S.P.: It's been 17 years since I lost my 21 year old daughter. I can be perfectly fine one minute and something or someone or a song whatever and it can bring me to tears and feeling my grief come to the top. It's like a wave, when the tide comes in you are calm; when the tide goes out it brings your grief right back up to the surface.

N.F.:…I still grieve 2 babies that I lost over 40 yrs ago…

J.B.: dads (go through it) too.

S.T.L.: It does get better but still happens…5 years out…. This past week we had a lot of snow….my son passed away during a snow storm I had a complete melt down…..

J.T.B.: It still happens after 10 years. Sometimes it scares me because my mood drops so drastically.

M.H.: *Grief is like an ocean, some days it's calm, and then there are days when a storm rages.. Every day is different. I'm a father. I lost my son 22 yrs ago, and there are still stormy days.*

A.H.: *I just hide mine and Idk why but I hide my break downs*

K.S.C.: *It is completely amazing to me (in a horrific way) how easy it is for something to make that feeling to occur. One minute you think you're handling things just fine and the next minute OUT OF NOWHERE you are laid low again. Like a big emotional bomb just exploded on you. And simple, little, trivial things can be the trigger...*

J.J.: *I came across his hair brush the other day and his hair is still in it. I sobbed and sobbed and slept with it.*

L.G.: *... My baby girl passed on Sept 6 1980 at 5 days old. Some days it still hits me like a Mack truck doing 80mph.*

R.R.: *I feel we have so much love for our child and when they were here we could express it to them daily, but now it can only build up in us and when our cup has runneth over it comes out in tears to make room for more love and thoughts for our child that we so dearly miss...*

L.P.: *I lost my son on 6-30-69 and I couldn't believe I would ever reach anywhere close to being normal. So, if normal is breaking into tears when I hear his favorite music, or catch a whiff of his favorite cologne, ponder over and over why did he have to be taken and so many still unanswered questions, well, then I'm as normal as I hope to be. I can function day to day. I do have off days still, but I love and miss my son from the moment I laid eyes on him as a baby, until the day of his wake and saying good-by at his funeral. ...we all lost a child that we helped make. How can we ever totally get over that? Never, but your coping skills will change.*

My husband wrote his thoughts on this subject in his chapter of my book *When Tragedy Strikes*.

I believe most of us men tend to compartmentalize everything in our minds. Mark Gungor (Laugh Your Way to a Better Marriage) says we have tiny little boxes that we take out ever so gently so as to not disturb any other boxes. I think this is a pretty accurate description of me. For the most part, I was able to take out my work box and stay there, but grief had just shattered my "Becca box" into a million pieces. I tried to sweep my grief into a grief box, but the problem with grief is that it cannot stay in a box! Somehow those shattered pieces find a way into all the other boxes. These pieces tend to appear out of nowhere and not always at convenient times.

It was not easy, and at times I would close my door and allow myself to tear up and grieve some more. So if you're reading this and you're a father who has lost a child and you tend to compartmentalize, I encourage you to allow yourself those moments to grieve. Grieving is not a sign of weakness, it is a way for us to heal.

Yes, we will be healing for the rest of our lives.

Words of Grace and Hope

J.M.D.: *...I cry out to Jesus for His help when my emotions are taking over. He is my peace and hiding place and my refuge.*
A.S.: *You will smile again and really mean it. You won't feel guilty for laughing either. I know it sounds hard... However I had to take down pictures and put away items that were constant reminders. I also removed every calendar in the house for a time. Once some time passed by, I was able to put the pictures back on the walls and enjoy them now. I explained it by comparing my grief to a broken bone. Bones need to be set in a cast for a while so the bone can heal... (There isn't a magic pill that can heal a broken bone overnight). Once the shock was over I slowly started my life again...Find a way to help others... Volunteer somewhere.... It doesn't have to be with people related to grief or your situation right now. But even volunteering at a homeless shelter or a food bank can help you. You can start getting out and giving back... You will meet some amazing people out there. Hang in there...*

CHAPTER 12

||||||||||

What About My Other Children?

Having one of our children leave this earth is shattering enough, but then we also have to get through the minefield of how our grief affects our other children, and how their grief as a sibling is often taken out on us. Unfortunately, there can be deep emotional casualties that go beyond the child who left this earth.

I have personally experienced the shock of this agonizing domino effect. In the past, our family has always allowed God to pull us close together, drawing our strength from Him and each other through any family crisis. But the death of my oldest daughter was a blow that has left one of our children splintered from the rest of the family (at least at the writing of this book). I have had to fight to not let it take me down for the count.

Even so, I refuse to judge anyone, parents, siblings, or grandparents for that matter, for how their pain has caused them to feel or react. I ask that you do the same, as the hearts of these parents are revealed to you in their place of immense pain.

> *L.P.S.: I had identical twin boys and then a daughter 13 months later. All three were very close growing up. My oldest son took his life July 2013…It breaks my heart every time my son comes to visit. I want to see him but it makes me so sad, knowing his brother is gone…Every holiday is terrible, knowing that he is missing from the table.*

B.M.: *You try to pull your love away because of fear of losing another and the pain you know that will be.*

J.W.: *I just recently lost my 14 yr old son to suicide. My 12 yr old son says he just wants to forget, & talking about it makes it worse. I find my 10 yr old daughter staring at pictures & crying, being angry. She was home when he did it & my 12 yr old spotted him first. We all saw the horror...*

C.G.D.: *Our daughter passed away April 2014 at age 35. Every time our son (two years younger), dropped by it took my breath away because seeing him just made me think more about not seeing her. Being the wonderful son he is, he picked up on this. He then made it a point to drop by almost daily, sit down and say, "let's talk about (daughter)." It's great, it helps us and him, in our grief journey. We have always been close, but this is bringing us even closer. I no longer lose my breath because it's like he is bringing (daughter) with him.*

S.J.: *I had a miscarriage on Mother's Day of all days, but I never stopped grieving and I REFUSED to do anything for Mother's Day. My child was grieving the loss of his brother or sister. (I never wanted to know the sex of my baby.) For YEARS we never did anything; for years while he was going to school he never made me anything for Mother's Day. My child's teacher asked my son why he didn't want to make me something for Mother's Day and they talked and he made me a gift. His 1st gift to me was in 4th grade and we both cried and shared a special day, and since then we still cry and have our special time every year, even though we are adults now.*

C.P.: *My son, 23 at the time, passed Feb 2013 and my now only living son has put space between us because I seem to talk about my son who passed. It breaks my heart but I'm trying to come to grips with this. I know he's also dealing with a lot, because that was his only brother.*

S.M.J.: *I hated myself for not wanting to spend quality time with my other son, it's still hard, but I try to remind myself that he lost his brother too and he needs his mom.*

G.S.:...*My younger daughter has a daughter who is the spitting image of my older daughter. I see her & sometimes it is*

What About My Other Children?

just too much...I have to fight with everything I have to keep from collapsing...

S.H.: For the first year after my son died, I had a hard time when being with his identical twin brother. (He died at 25). And my first granddaughter, born a month before (son) died - oh, I missed that first year of bonding with her. I was just so sad because her birth, and having only 1/2 of my matching set, just really brought the grief out. My remaining son, now 35, is cherished by me because every once in a while I can still hear (son's) voice and laugh in his, and I will always have (son) around when his twin is near... I am so glad both my husband and I held on and worked our way through some of the worst days of our lives, and that we still have our 1/2 of the matching set in physical form, and two lovely granddaughters.

C.R.A.: I actually get anxiety when the other 3 kids want to have a family get-together. It is getting a bit better because I force myself to do it and I cry if I have to. I also have a difficult time getting together with my siblings and seeing them so happy with their children while I always have that huge hole that I know will never be filled. What has helped a lot is now I have 3 little grandbabies to cuddle and love.

S.J.: I've been told by my daughter I loved her dead brother more which isn't so. She has no idea what it's like...

D.D.: ... our whole family structure changed to being distant and uncaring.

K.F.C.: I was blessed with 6 boys. My 2nd born took his life at the age of 22... Losing him shattered us all, and still is. I still have a terrible time being around any of the other kids. I look at them and all I feel is total loss. The holidays are torturous when they all get together, as there should be 9, not 8...nobody is happy, nobody is close anymore. I have tried my best to keep everyone together, but the pain is too severe. We all hardly even talk anymore. It feels like I've lost all of my children...but in a sense, I guess we all lost a huge part of us when (son) left.

L.G.: *I still feel uncomfortable around my 29 year old daughter. My son is a different story; we talk about (son) all the time and visit his grave....*

J.M.: *When I lost a son it was months till I realized what I was doing. It was only when I was talking to my other son one day... he said mom, this is the first time you've spoken to me since (son) died. I said no, it's not. He said yeah. You will say things like your tea is ready, or your washing is there, etc., but this is the first proper conversation.*

E.M.S.: *The moment I knew my son was medically declared dead I freaked. It was all about me. He was my boy. I loved him so! My older son stopped me in my tracks when he said: Mom I only had one brother. His eyes pierced me with grief. I looked at all three siblings and realized we were a family in this together...I was not the only one that loved the little boy that died. He belonged to all of us in different ways.*

C.H.E.: *I lost my oldest son, (name), he was 14 at the time, and my youngest son was 11. I wanted to die, but I couldn't. I think of it like this; my oldest son is safe in the cave, and my youngest is out in the woods alone... Who NEEDS you? I have come to realize how precious my living child is to me.*

M.L.: *My son, the middle child of 3, died of suicide in 2008 when he was 18... I was so frightened of losing his siblings through possible estrangement, but we all worked very hard with counseling and patience and are closer now than ever.*

C.S.F.: *I lost one of my 8 yr old triplet boys about 20 months ago. I had two identical and one that was not, and looked completely opposite of his identical brothers. I lost the one that was not identical. It took me a whole year before I could be any kind of a mother to his brothers. They just seem to go on so easily and I resented that, not that I wanted them to suffer as I was, but still...I just kept thinking I'll never know what he would have looked like all grown up... I also can't stand any type of family gathering and hate to even go out to eat or anywhere with my boys because one is missing and strangers refer to them as "twins"... I depend on prayers from other people because I can't even seem to pray any more. It just seems*

> *so unfair. I've tried grief therapy but still felt alone in a room full of people.*
> F.P.D.W.: *My other sons refuse to talk about their oldest brother. One of our last encounters was one of them saying he was a coward for taking his own life. I have not seen or spoken to him for that in over 5 yrs. now.*
> J.L.H.: *My daughter thinks I loved my son more than her. I feel betrayed by my family. My daughter and my husband are very close. They both think I shouldn't still be grieving. She calls her dad, but never calls me. I feel like the black sheep. She has two boys, and the oldest looks so much like my son that died, but I don't get to see them but about once a week… I feel like I've lost both of my children, and my husband doesn't seem to grieve like I do.*

Grief is such an ugly thing. God did not create death. Death is the result of the enemy bringing sin into the world. And the enemy is right there to continue doing as much damage as possible in our pain of dealing with the loss of our child.

We desperately need your prayers of protection and love over our families, in all areas, physically, emotionally, and spiritually. Thank you.

Words of Grace and Hope

> T.J.: *We are four years into our grief and can say honestly that there is joy and laughter again. We have a surviving son and just recently sat around the table with him and laughed, all of us, naturally and spontaneously. Early grief is so brutal…It took me a long to time to realize that love never dies, the love that filled your home will be there, always.*
> J.O.: *…My son was such a rock, he would have protected my right to grieve any way I wanted and I wanted him to have his mom back! We knew that would not happen overnight, but he was patient…When grief was the newest, maybe that whole first year, my biggest question to my son was, "can we even survive this?" and I'm sure he was scared and he was also*

broken, he would hold me and say, "mom, we are going to survive this, I don't know how we will live without (son/brother) but we will!"

CHAPTER 13

||||||||||

We Lost Our Only Child

I have had discussions with other bereaved moms where we all agree, when we hear the story of how someone else lost their child, we can't imagine losing a child *that* way. I am sure that might sound strange, but somehow it is how we feel.

Along with that, I cannot even begin to imagine what it would be like to face the darkness of losing my only child, or all of my children; to never again hear anyone call me Mom. And I am sure there are those who don't even consider you a parent any more since you don't have children on this earth. How utterly devastating, to lose all of that in one moment of time, as this pareavor describes.

> *We lost our 15-year-old daughter this past August, suddenly. She was our only child. I have so many bad days and feel like I need to put on a 'mask' every time I'm out in the real world. When I'm home alone I cry all the time and miss the little things she used to do… like come out of her room and ask what's for dinner, etc. I always feel alone and empty and more anxious then I ever have. Her father and I are heartbroken, but are always there for each other, but I can't get over how I feel inside… I feel so lost and alone without her. I'm always tired and I never have any motivation. I miss hearing her call me 'momma' and her dad 'daddio. My heart just aches. (Source unknown.)*

And yet these parents are so very willing to reach out to others who suddenly find themselves in this same place. Let's take a peek at how they relate to one another and also offer words of encouragement to others who find themselves in this unimaginable place.

C.D.J.: We tragically lost our only child, our son in July of 2011 at age 11...Losing an only child is different ... Please be very gentle with yourself. Don't allow anyone in your bubble that makes you feel worse, even if they think they are trying to help. It's about you and your husband. There's also a page called Grieving Moms Without Surviving Children on Facebook. It's where I've gotten a lot of support...

S.Y.: I lost my only child at 17, seven years ago and it's still very hard; there is a huge void. The mask is so true, but I've learned when I'm not having a good day or not feeling like being bothered I don't. I let myself feel whatever I'm feeling. The Mask as bereaved parents is unhealthy. We don't owe the world a smile. You owe yourself time to grieve.

L.C.B.K.: I lost my only child last August. He was just 29 and I am broken. I don't know how to function on a daily basis. Sometimes I sit down and all of a sudden I realize I haven't moved for hours. I feel like I haven't got a future because all happy memories are in the past and he's no longer here to make any more. You never think you're going to lose your child; it's such a heartbreaking time for myself and his dad.

T.D.: ...I stayed awake for days, was hospitalized for a week because my mind and body was shutting down. It wasn't until I was on the right medication that I started functioning again.

J.B.C.: I talk about him every chance I get...He was my only child and everything to me. I lost him on Christmas Eve, 1996 to a car accident. He was coming home from college for the Holidays. The knock on the door should have been him, not the Sheriff with the news. My world and life has never been the same. There is an emptiness that no one or anything can fill.

P.D.J.: I lost my only child suddenly at 15, July 3, 1996, who also then had her 16th birthday in Dec. She was my life as I was a single parent for 13 of her years...One of the first things

We Lost Our Only Child

I learned was that drinking, drugs/meds will only prolong your grief. We have to work thru it....there's no getting around it.

K.A.: It's been a year for me. She was 16. We lost her 4 days after Christmas. I still jump up and think she's late for school. My anxiety is so high. I write to her every day, it helps. I keep a journal and I still do all her favorite things. Everyone is picking out prom dresses and I'm putting together flowers for her grave. I'm not going to say it gets easier, just different. I think talking to others who have lost their child helps me. My heart is missing and I have no energy to love. My marriage failed due to this. So I'm all alone now...Find something she loved and start doing it. My (daughter) loved (a certain product) so I now sell it. It keeps me very busy and I love it. But at the end of the day it all comes back. I pray for you and your family and I hope someday you can find some peace

A.J.D.: I lost my daughter 5 years ago in a car accident. The grief process is a long trip with no shortcuts. I had PTSD so bad that I was displaying symptoms similar to schizophrenia. Thoughts of my daughter consumed my every waking moment and I was like some kind of zombie on "auto pilot." She was my first thought when I woke up and my last thought before falling asleep. Finally after about 4 years, a small miracle happened and she was the *second* thought I had upon waking. The grief had not gone away but it had finally allowed a little room in my heart and mind to consider something other than just her.

P.G.W.: Our son was our one and only -- that was 6 years ago -- and initially I had these horrible panic/anxiety attacks -- my doctor prescribed a medication....and I used it on an as needed basis... after 6 years, I feel as if my husband & I have reinvented ourselves.......so different now from 6 years ago....we live with that loss, it will never leave, but we live a good life, one my son would be proud of.

L.G.: After losing our son in Dec. of 2012 I would sit and cry and my whole body would shake with the grief. I would see him everywhere. I can still hear his voice in my head. My husband and I were always there for each other and still are.

B.B.: ... *I lost my two kids in a fire and it was the worst pain ever...I know you don't think it will, but it will get better, I PROMISE you that. But don't let anyone tell you how you should be feeling now; you need to feel that hurt.*

Y.C.: *I lost both my boys and it hurts every day! Today is a bad day for me; tears since I woke up for them and other things in my life... find someone to talk to, to share your pain and not be judged.*

J.H.: *I have also lost my only child (daughter) who was 6 weeks short of turning 20 when she lost a 15 month battle with cancer. I also lost my husband to cancer when she was only 3. I have just had (daughter's) 7 year anniversary yesterday and it was the first time I was able to post a photo on Facebook. Her room is still as it was when she passed. I still have her purse in my bag. There are so many more things with the loss of an only child, including never having grandchildren. I have had no one to lean on and it has been like a double grief for me as I don't think I really grieved for my husband as I had my daughter to concentrate on.*

If ever a parent needed words of grace and hope, it is these precious ones.

Words of Grace and Hope

T.L.B.: *It's an awful pain. My 20 year old son went to get his paycheck July 5 last year and never came back. A van turned in front of his motorcycle. If it had not been for the Lord... (Ps124) He gives me strength and hope and He is the reason I live. He gives strength to the weak, and to them that have no might He increases strength. I have bad days... Yes, I do. But instead of sorrowing that my (son) is no longer here on this earth, I rejoice that we had him as long as we did.*

S.M.C.: *Death of our child is such a personal journey, a journey we never dreamed we would take. (Daughter) has been gone for 19 months; my only child. She gave me great joy and I miss her beyond words. (Daughter) was not my only joy. I have struggled thru God's love, mercy, and grace, knowing she is not dead. I will hold her again, and we will share laughter as we always did. God has led me to peace, in knowing she saw so much and did so much; to remember what she saw, not what she won't see. It has been a daily struggle to keep my mind and heart focused on my blessing...God gave me such a wonderful gift - she called me Mom...God promised each of us a homecoming day. That promise keeps me looking forward to each new day...*

CHAPTER 14

What Does "Family" Mean to Me Now?

"A child's death forever changes a family and those who love them. The experience of grief is life-long – it does not go away after a certain amount of time. Yes, it softens, but always there is a place in your heart and your soul that yearns for that child." (Anonymous.)

When we have to say a final goodbye to our child, it affects everything. The word "family" takes on a whole new meaning. Our family will never be complete again. There are no replacements for child loss. Ever. And because of that, phrases with the word family in them can bring on crashing emotions.

- Family photo
- Family reunion
- Family vacation
- Family meal
- Family pack (of tickets, etc.)
- Family holiday
- Family picnic

Any kind of family gathering, event, or even advertisements, is a glaring reminder of the child we are missing.

So many events become bittersweet. Our middle son will be the only one of the siblings who had all five of them present at his wedding. The other four will be missing their sister, both at the event, and in the family wedding photos. Bittersweet…

We have had two grandchildren born since Becca died. The day those precious little girls made their entrance into the world was wonderful, but someone was missing. We only have one grandchild who knew her Aunt Becca. These other two granddaughters, and any other grandchildren we have, will not have that blessing. Bittersweet...

Our family is growing, and as my children get married and start their own families, it gets harder to have us all together for the holidays. On those fun times when we are all together, we aren't really all together, because Becca and her daughter are missing. Bittersweet...

Graduations, school dances, Mother's Day and Father's Day, birthday parties, weddings, baby showers...all of these and many more events can be overshadowed with a reminder of who is not there, and be bittersweet...

We have to do our best to choose to focus on the blessings we have, and lean into the sweet, instead of the bitter, but it can be extremely difficult (especially if the birthday or anniversary date falls during any of those time-frames).

It helps, when the family makes sure the memory of our child is kept alive at these events.

> *S.S.V.: I'm always here 24/7 for you and my nephews. We will always keep his memories going and will keep passing them down from our children to their children to their children. It'll never stop, I promise you my sister, love you.*
>
> *J.J.: It's a struggle daily. Thanksgiving was both of my brothers' favorite holiday. They loved their food and loved the time the entire family got together for family time. It's not the same...Holidays for me are really just another day to get through. I realized the more I wished for the day to be over, and praying the next day would be better, that I am letting my days slip away. We are not promised tomorrow so I must learn how to live if for none other than my grandchildren. Since my brothers' deaths my mom keeps her distance. I guess it's easier for her not to feel guilty that way because I am her only*

surviving child. She turns away from me; I don't know but it hurts a lot. She gets mad because my kids don't call her but she is never available. She hasn't gone to any of the great grandkids' birthdays either. I miss her. She also knows I have a hard time with my older brother's death. I haven't accepted it because of the trauma he went through. He died looking me in the eye while holding my hand.

K.C.: Family gatherings are so hard. I don't enjoy them whatsoever.

A.L.: Does anyone else find it hard to be happy for someone who is expecting when your heart is permanently broken??

L.K.: I'll never be the same. Like I've said before I HATE the holidays. My family will never be complete neither will my heart. I have forever been broken.

V.C.: I lost my 12 yr old son 11-20-11 from a go cart accident in our front yard. I have celebrated the first Thanksgiving and Christmas without him but spent it still numb from the shock. In 7 days I will encounter not only the anniversary of his death but be thrown into the holiday season actually feeling his loss. I am trying to be strong but can feel panic, sadness, and want to withdraw but I also have his 2 younger brothers and father to help them thru. I know I have a strong God to carry me thru but I miss (son) soooo much!

P.K.: It has been three years, and when I hear of the ones around me talking about doing or seeing things with their family, it still just sends me into a roller coaster.

S.L.: For me, it isn't always the date itself, be it birthday, holiday, death date. The days leading up to the date are often harder for me, and the out-of-the-blue-knock-me-to-my-knees-days are hardest of all, and can be triggered by something as innocuous as feeling the sun on my shoulders… The hardest days I've lived with in the past almost five years (besides the initial shock and despair) following my daughter's murder? When her younger siblings caught up to, and then passed her in age.

Yes, our family will never be complete this side of heaven. But someday...

Words of Grace and Hope

B.C.: My son, 32, died June 30, 2014...heart attack in his sleep....It has been the most excruciating painful months since his passing! What keeps me going? What brings me joy and laughter during this nightmarish journey? It is my faith in God. He sustains me. He is my strength! Without Him I would crumble up into a ball and die! It is God's promises and His assurance of a beautiful Heaven full of life and my son that keeps me focused on my eternity. We ALL must step into this eternity someday - I know I will see my son again and this alone brings me comfort and joy!

D.S.: Oh, please know that there is HOPE!! It's been almost 12 years since our 16yr old son (name) died in a car accident, and the first year was really hard, BUT, we knew that to fully honor him, we had to be the parents that he knew, not only for him but for our older son. I feel we have recreated our lives. Yes, there is a part missing, but we have joy and laughter and tears and sorrow and joy and laughter......We also have 2 lovely grandsons, and life goes on.

CHAPTER 15

|||||||||

Year One, Year Two, Year Three, and Beyond

Any loss takes time to process and work through. The loss of a loved one can take weeks, months, and years. The loss of a child takes a lifetime.

Grief has its own individual path for each person. We may often hear the words, "There is no right or wrong way to grieve," and yet society as a whole shouts the exact opposite to those who are in deep mourning.

"I feel like I need to say this to the parents who are still in deep grief. Do *not* look at any dates to see where I or others were emotionally in our grieving process and use it as some sort of a timeline to force on yourself. We are all on our own individual timeline and need to go through the process at our own speed. Yes, there are some 'patterns' (for lack of a better word) that some of us seem to fall into, but don't expect yourself to fit into that. Give yourself grace to walk your own necessary path. As long as you are putting one foot in front of the other, you will get there."
(Quote from my book *When Tragedy Strikes*.)

But...as I started hearing from other bereaved parents, I discovered there seems to be an underlying generic time-frame that many of us pareavors sort of fall into.

The first year is a painful fog, full of numbness, confusion, pain, and disbelief. All of the "firsts" hit us hard. The first time he or she is not with us for *each* holiday or yearly family event, the first year they are not here for their birthday, and of course the first anniversary of their death.

I thought the second year would be easier, because I had already gone through everything once. As pareavors just starting out on this horrific journey, we don't think it is even possible, but the second year of being without our child is usually worse than the first year. That first year I braced myself for all of the "firsts," plus I was still in that fog of trying to figure out if this had really happened. The second year caught me off guard as the fog began to lift. When that initial shock finally wears off, it causes the weight of our loss to hit us full force, with a heaviness and darkness that leaves us wondering if we will be able to live through it. Round two of all those yearly events no longer has the blessing of numbness to block the full depth of the pain.

The third year for many of us becomes more livable. We are starting to accept the finality and painful fact that our child will never again be with us at any of these events. We are starting to resign ourselves to the fact that no matter how much it hurts, we must figure out who we are without our child. Some of us begin to see glimmers of hope, that we can still have joy and happiness in the life we are living with those who are still here whom we love, and who love us.

Unfortunately though, there many parents who are stuck in the second "level." They take many more years to get to the place of painful acceptance, which is necessary, to be able to start building their new normal in a way that brings peace, joy, love, and laughter back into their lives.

Here are what other parents have to say on what the first few years are like after the death of their child. As you will see, many will confirm this three year "timeline," but there are still plenty who do not.

> *G.H.M.: It has been 6 1/2 years since we lost our daughter and that 2nd year was the worst. I find each year brings a little more healing.*
>
> *K.D.P.: I just passed anniversary #5 in Dec. For me, year 1 - I hardly remember anything, mainly a fog. Year 2 (for me) was worse. The numbness was gone. It was real. It was crushing. I*

survived day-to-day. Year 3 -I started feeling some joy again. Able to go a few days without crying. Year 4 - still painful, but more like a slap than a body-slam.

L.D.: *I lost mine 25 years ago and I completely agree with this time line. My son and his wife are about to face the 1st angelversary of their 2 year old's passing. It has been a long hard gut-wrenching year. My son has been in such a deep depression. He has been waiting for this 1st Anniversary to pass so he can begin to function normally again. I don't have the heart to tell him that the worst year is about to begin.*

T.B.A.: *The FIVE year mark was my hardest yet. But I pushed through about four months into it (around the time the seasons changed outside).*

C.M.M.: *Time will be your enemy and best friend...Four years later, I still struggle with these feelings but not on a daily basis....*

J.L.M.: *July will mark year 5. I honestly couldn't tell you anything about the first 2 years. My oldest daughter started preschool during that time and I almost feel as if she got cheated because I wasn't mentally here. Year 3 things began to get a little better. We began to make a new normal. Not saying we forgot (daughter) because Lord knows I still cry every day. Year 4 I smiled again. Real smiles, not forced ones. And just over the past few months I have finally begun to feel happiness. You never forget. But you do make a new normal. One that includes memories and smiles.*

A.F.: *I was in shock, pain, and pretty much numb year one. Years two and three were when real grief started. Shock had subsided, numbness wore off, people were getting on with their lives, I began to feel, really feel, and know that (daughter) wasn't coming back. This wasn't a nightmare dream, it was real. I had a daughter for almost 30 yrs and now no daughter...There is no magic solution or remedy...The journey is daunting. You have two choices when your child dies, only two. You go on and live the journey and be the best you can be for her, or you don't...*

C.K.M.: *My son passed away from Strep Throat. I still wonder if this is all real. I said to my husband yesterday, "did we really have a son named (son)?" It is so unimaginable to lose a child; I doubt I will ever fully get it and will likely never accept it. Before you think I am psychotic... I do know it is all real... BUT... how could this possibly happen?*

C.H.: *I pretended my youngest son moved out to Denver to be with my eldest son. I think our minds do these things to save our sanity until eventually enough time passes and the shock and numbness wears off enough to deal with reality. My son died 4 years ago. Mostly I'm okay, but every so often I have a complete meltdown.*

N.B.A.: *It's been seven and a half years for us. Every. Single. Day. I have to convince myself it's real. The hole in my heart is still as big as the first day. Some days the pain is nearly unbearable. You will NEVER accept the fact that your child is dead. You learn to survive each day as it comes. It's never easy.*

B.P.: *Five years later I still deal with these issues. My daughter was 43 and lived in a different city, so I lived a lot of my life with her being on her own. Sometimes it's easy to think she's just living away from home and I catch myself thinking that she'll be home soon for a visit. Then I have to come to grips with the fact that this is for the rest of my life. I have no memory of the first year, but the next year was terrible. I could hardly move, and the pain...never have I felt so forsaken and alone.*

N.W.J.: *At first I experienced waves of grief that crashed over me throwing me prostrate to the floor in agony. After 3-4 years it was mostly a gentle longing with times of intense pain and feelings of loss. Even 44 years after the loss of my child I still on occasion feel the waves.*

J.A.B.: *For me denial was a big thing...if I did not acknowledge he was gone ... and I was looking for him around every corner.....then I pushed to accept it at 1 year - BIG MISTAKE.....we are 3 1/2 years and some days it is difficult and I hold tight to his memories and just breathe deeply and push through the day! Year 1 was in a fog, year 2 was harder but for me the 3rd year hit hard as it became a reality and his birthday was on Mother's day!*

K.M.W.: Some days I really feel like I am losing my mind and have to really focus so it doesn't completely leave me. Year 2 is worse. But I am intentionally seeking Joy and now I'm halfway through the second year. I think I can see Joy every now and then although it is still a ways ahead of me yet.

L.H.: Our new reality becomes our never ending nightmare. I am going on year 6 that I lost my younger son at 18 to cancer… not a day goes by that I do not miss him with all my heart! Sadly, the only way to 'get past this' is to go through it!! I am broken now in a place that will never heal. But I do find that I can laugh more than I used to, but I define my life 'before my son died' and 'after he died.' When a child dies, the parent buries them in their heart…trying to reach down into our memories and remember the scent of their hair…their bright shining faces…how it felt to hug them…all things we will never experience again!! We all loved our children with all our heart…so losing them is something we will grieve for the rest of our lives. The trick is to wake up every day and try to have a plan and a purpose.

L.B.: I lost my 17 year old daughter 6 1/2 years ago and I still can't accept it. It is something I struggle with every single day. It has made me such an angry person and I don't like who I am anymore. The sad thing is that I don't know how to change myself.

J.M.M.: I heard something one morning and it might help you. It was whispered to me, "every day you wake up is another day closer to being with him again," and you know what? Whoever said that to me is right. So now every day I wake up, I repeat those words, and every night I got to bed, knowing I am another day closer to seeing my son again.

Year one, year two, year three, year five, year ten, year twenty, the rest of this life time…and then comes our glorious reunion.

Words of Grace and Hope

L.H.: It is so hard to accept the reality. My daughter was 14 when she died 11 yrs and 7 months ago. It's not fair, we weren't done. We needed proms, boyfriends, weddings, grandbabies. I said out loud to God what I thought about this, and then I relinquished my caring for her to Him. The biggest hurdle I had was reminding myself that she was His to begin with; our job was to give them what we could while they were with us.

J.K.M.: Tight hugs to parents who must wake without their child. It's been 7 years without my daughter, who died at age 10. There are mornings I can still smell her hair, hear her loud laugh, and recall the morning grumpiness. With childlike FAITH, I focus on the fact that each day I manage the emptiness of her.... I'm 1 day closer to being with her!

CHAPTER 16

A Commercial That Blindsided Us

I wasn't going to include this, but the more I thought about it, the more I realized it needed to be in here. Let me explain. As I was writing this book, the 2015 Super Bowl happened. And what is the best part about the Super Bowl? The commercials, of course (unless the Packers are in it)! All across America, TVs are tuned in for a fun day with family and friends to watch this yearly highlight.

This year, as we watched it from our living room, there was a commercial that stunned our family to the very core. I fought tears as we sat and stared at each other in shock and disbelief. Was it because of extreme sexual content? No. Was there some horrific scene of violence? No. It was an insurance company, trying to raise awareness of preventable childhood accidents.

So what is so disturbing about that? So glad you asked. They did it by showing a little boy describing the life he will never have, because he died in a childhood accident (and it had scenes such as an open cupboard door under the sink with exposed poisons, a bathtub with overflowing water, a TV on the floor, etc.). Unless you are a bereaved parent, you probably would think it was a good commercial.

Parental grief organizations (and the insurance company) were *immediately* flooded with emails, social media comments, and calls, from those who were offended or deeply hurt by the ad. They felt it was extremely insensitive to us families who are grieving the death of our children.

A grief organization that has a Facebook page specifically for grieving parents, asked how they felt about this ad. *There were well over 1000 responses within a few short hours!* I actually went through every single one of them. Out of the responses from the parents themselves, 28% had no problem with it, 19% had mixed feelings, and 53% were shocked, devastated, and angered, leaving them picking up the pieces the rest of the night for themselves or even worse, their other children. (In other words, it rattled almost 3 out of every 4 pareavors.) There were also thousands of responses in other places from the same "audience."

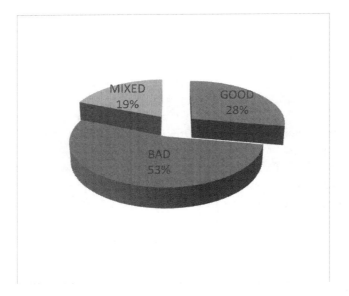

I had a really hard time chopping down the responses into a reasonably short chapter. Here is what is left after three rounds of editing it down.

If you would like to watch the forty-eight second commercial before hearing from these parents, it can be found on YouTube by typing in your search bar, "Nationwide

A Commercial That Blindsided Us

2015 Super Bowl Commercial" (as of the publishing of this book, anyway).

> *D.D.S: My husband and I sat there in shock! He immediately had tears running down his face. My jaw just hung open. We know our son won't have the chance to marry, or to wear a tux, or have children, and all the other things many of our children won't be able to do. But to see it like that?!!!! It was horrendous! Our son was killed riding an ATV where someone had put a steel cable at neck height on a paved road. He never saw it. How could it have been prevented? Of course, if we could find the people that put it up then I can show them the commercial, I guess. I was up crying all night. Even if there is nothing that a parent could have done to save their child, there is not a parent that doesn't feel guilty about it. God forbid, if you happened to turn your head for a second and something happened....SHAME on this insurance company!*
>
> *A.A.W.: I have been with nationwide 11+ yrs and at no point have they ever asked if I have small children in my home or directed me to go to a safety site. I receive 2-3 mailings a month from them and have NEVER received anything about child safety. Then yesterday this commercial showed up. It is a ploy to get customers. If they were that concerned about child safety you would think they would start with their own policy holders. They had another option for the commercial and chose the one that aired. I did not sleep last night with my mind racing about all things my son would never do. I'm now looking for new ins company.*
>
> *R.P.: I lost my son 2 1/2 years ago. The Super Bowl was very special to us, his friends would come over, I'd make all kinds of snacks etc. I knew it was going to be a grief ridden day. So I tried and went to a Super Bowl party locally. When I saw that commercial, everyone there immediately looked at me. I was in absolute horror. I could not believe what I was seeing. I had to get up and leave, all I could think of was my son being killed in a car accident at 16.*

J.&R.B: *Someone suggested a hashtag for Instagram: #mylossisnotyourcommercial*

P.L.: *My child died in a preventable accident, but I think the commercial probably saved lives. I was not upset or offended at all.*

L.C.M.: *This was a major PTSD trigger for many children as well as adults who are struggling to cope with the very reality their marketing department shoved down our throats at an otherwise family oriented gathering... Thanks a lot, Nationwide...where are you now? By our children's sobbing sides?*

M.E.G.S.: *The Super Bowl traditionally is such a festive event and one that doesn't stir up memories of my daughter. I was actually enjoying myself when that commercial hit. The group I was with didn't know what to say. I felt unsettled the rest of the night...They basically took the deepest fear of every parent who has lost a child and said it was valid. It's your fault...*

P.M.: *I think it was the right message, but the wrong approach. Nationwide had NO IDEA how many grieving parents they blindsided with that commercial. I was furious, I cried... I didn't appreciate them exploiting a dead child to get a point across. We already know what our child will not get to do. It was a smack in the face.*

T.S.W.: *I witnessed the killing of my child by a negligent school bus driver in front of my home and suffer from flashbacks all the time. This ad is sad, but it is a voice for these children who have been killed in "accidents." Maybe the reminder should be given to us more often, lest we forget what took our precious children in the first place. Through pain comes triumph. Let it make you mad and hurt, and then do something to prevent these "accidents."*

L.B.P.: *I had the worst attack full blown PTSD episode. I am terrified that they will air it again and I will go through it again publicly or when I have my grandkids. My flashbacks had me right there all over again. I could feel her lips so cold, heard my other kids, watched myself doing CPR, it was BAD! We want to make sure they never play it again. Not like that!!!!!*

A Commercial That Blindsided Us

C.M.B.: *...Here I am, enjoying the nail-biter game...enjoying all the other commercials, discussing each with my husband. Then...I ran headlong into a brick wall. I went numb for a moment... For a splice of time I was right back there...holding my beautiful (daughter)...my stomach wrenched in knots... Breathe. I had to remind myself to breathe. Bad taste... Shame on you, Nationwide! Whose side are you really on?*

P.RF.G.: *With the way people treat child loss as some taboo subject that should never be openly discussed, I'm kind of glad that they aired it. Child loss IS horrifying. It hurts, it destroys, it tears you apart. If a commercial can make someone think about it, and what they might be able to do to avoid becoming a member to this heart breaking "club," then I'm all for it.*

C.M.M.: *It was a festive atmosphere in our house...our beloved New England Patriots were in the Super Bowl! Once that commercial aired, we were stunned and silent. We felt like we were punched in the stomach. I thought it was the most cruel, insensitive advertisement. To sell insurance based on a parent's worst fear is disgusting to say the least. My son drowned while working....he lost control of a mower and ended up at the bottom of a pond with the machine pinning him. It was a tragic accident...could it have been preventable?? I still don't have the answer...but the guilt that we struggle with never leaves us. Shame on you, Nationwide....You didn't factor in the audience that this is now their reality.*

M.M.: *The point is we don't need to be reminded our children won't graduate high school, they won't get married, they won't have children... That's the part of the commercial that was way over the line. If you want to save lives by reminding people to safe guard their homes that's fine but do it in a tasteful way, not by making people relive the nightmare of losing their child and what they will never get to experience.*

K.L.R.: *I lost my youngest 3 years ago, he too will never experience these things. To be honest the ad did affect me, but I would much rather be the person telling my story and saving a life. I was naive before losing my son, it was one of those things* that are mentioned but you think 'that won't happen to me,' then it does.

T.M.H.: It made me catch my breath for a minute. I guess I understand that they were trying to get a message out to the most people possible. I honestly have mixed feelings.

M.C.: As a parent to a child that died in an accident 3 yrs ago it heaped more guilt on top of the guilt I already had.

D.M.: As a parent who lost an adult child to illness I am so glad that someone has finally started to talk about child death. It is not spoken about, ever. It should be. If that commercial saves only one family from the loss of a child then it is worth all the controversy and anger!!

D.B.C.: It took my breath away & my mind went right back to my son's accident. I don't feel they meant to be insensitive or offensive. However, as parents who have experienced the agony of burying our babies, another reminder of how our child won't see graduation, or marriage, or 9 years old hurts. It will always hurt, because not only did our babies miss these milestones, so did we.

K.G.L.: Commercializing on a parent's worst nightmare is reprehensible. And for those of us living that nightmare, the ad was cruel. Nationwide's purpose was to raise awareness for one thing...their brand. If it was truly a community service ad, then leave the blue logo off the screen and don't say your brand in the voiceover. The ad served to outrage many, but to others it was a reinforcement of the guilt we live with every moment. Not all accidents are preventable...that's why they are called accidents. It can't all be foreseen. Sometimes, you just never know. It was tasteless and inappropriate for the audience the event drew. Shame on them.

B.D.J.: If their goal was to reach a large audience then they succeeded. As a parent who lost a child it is hard to watch but, if one parent is spared the pain I am suffering from, then it was good.

T.H.: I was in the middle of eating dinner when it came on. I could not even swallow the food in my mouth. I felt completely blindsided. I don't need reminders of how my son's death was preventable. I have thought of that every day for 11 years now.

K.O.: *I think it was insensitive to those of us who have lost children. But I think there was a higher purpose to it rather than insensitivity. I think it was geared more toward those who haven't lost children in an effort to prevent them from joining the club no one wants to join. And for that I would be willing to endure 60 seconds of pain.*

D.M.: *lost a child 27 yrs ago and still grieve. I like the ad. Why would someone be offended? How can it bring back pain? It never leaves.*

M.E.C.: *I would have preferred that they spread awareness by talking about their page where they educate parents about all the safety hazards there are around the home and vehicles. I went to their "make safe happen" website and they do list and educate about safety hazards... did they have to remind us grieving parents of all the things our kids are missing out on now that they are gone? All the things they will never do? It's a slap in the face. How about spreading awareness of things you shouldn't say to a grieving parent also? Good intentions or not, some damage was done.*

A.V.M.: *I hated it... made me think the rest of the game about the worst day of my life. Child death should not be used as a marketing tool to sell stupid insurance.*

H.H.: *If the ad makes someone think about their child's safety then I am willing to shed a few tears about my own loss.*

B.S.: *Did anyone stop to think that some of the members of the ad team could be parents of a child that was killed or harmed or has passed on? No parent should suffer the loss of a child in any way, but it's life and no matter what happens from day to day, grief and memories can be triggered. Lighten up on Nationwide, the ad wasn't meant to cause more pain.*

J.T.F.: *I lost a son to SIDS. I don't take it offensively at all because I am a mother to 5 children left on this planet that I need to protect from the what if's*

L.L.: *... I gasped and cried at the commercial then felt sick with the knowledge that (daughter) missed some of those same* things. During the SB is a time to touch the biggest audience and there is no better advertising than to stir up a controversy. Was it distasteful? Yeah. Did it make me sad? YEAH. Did it get my attention? Yeah. Did it make parents of young children stop and think? I HOPE SO! If it did then the ones of us that were hurt by it have a way to say it was worth my pain to save lives.

T.B.P.: I was shocked! I couldn't believe it! And it left me with a sick feeling in my gut. Then when someone started talking about it in the office the next day I had to get up and leave!

B.L.: ...The vision of an overflowing, unattended bathtub created an image that does not relate to reality, and portrays anyone who has lost a child accidentally as irresponsible. You have treated people who are already suffering from the greatest loss anyone can have with disregard, and added to their already overwhelming sense of grief. Your goal of starting a dialog on this issue discards those who are already suffering...Our disgust on seeing that ad was immediate, overwhelming, and opened wounds that were beginning to heal. We belong to a club that no one else wants to join. We didn't need your "cause" to further separate us from the rest of the world.

T.T.: My son died in an accident in our home 8 years ago. I wasn't offended. I think people need to know it's a reality. I surely never thought it would happen to my son. However, had I seen that same commercial earlier in the grieving process, I know I would have been offended and hurt.

That last comment seems to do a good job of summing up my thoughts about our reactions. Those whose grief was the freshest seemed the most upset. However, as you have also read, it caused lots of melt downs and grief attacks from "seasoned" parents to the grief.

This is actually a great lead into the next *very* important chapter. How can you help us?

Words of Grace and Hope

A.K.: As a parent who lost a child due to an accident (unattached bathrobe belt asphyxiation) I thought it was well done...a great reminder to parents that there are hazards out there. It did tug at my heart strings cause it reminds us grieving parents of the things our children won't do in their lifetimes. But I feel it is an educational ad for parents. When my (son) passed away it was my family's goal to educate parents on unattached bathrobe belts, now thanks to hard work it's actually a recommendation to manufactures to have the belt attached.

B.B.: It hurt and brought back memories, but I rather have a short relapse if it helps another parent. Sometimes the obvious is not always obvious. I have a younger son who is 4 at home and I'm very protective of him, but I realized my TV is not secured to the wall and I keep my cleaning products under my sink. I would rather hurt for a little than read an article in the paper about another parent who lost their child. We need to raise the awareness of child loss so it is not so taboo in this culture

CHAPTER 17

How Can You Help Someone Who Lost Their Child?

Some of you may have turned to this chapter first, wanting the information offered here right away. Let me be really blunt and up front. If you are hoping to find a checklist, so that you can mark something off to be able to put a notch in your "I care" belt, then please put the book down and walk away.

However, I believe most of you are reading this book because you know a pareavor, and you sincerely want to know how to help them. And if you want to start with this chapter, that is fine. But before you put anything you read in this chapter into action, I highly suggest you pick *at least* three chapters ahead of this one and read them, before implementing anything. (Reading all of them would be even better.)

Why do I say that? Because you will get much further with the precious parent you want to reach out to, if you have a better sense of our reality. If you have some insight into the swirling emotional upheaval we are in, you will be able to go from just sympathy to compassionate caring. Believe me, we know the difference, and many of us don't have the energy to waste on someone who is just sympathetic.

It is *extremely* rare for anyone who has not experienced the death of a child to have empathy or compassion at a level that can reach us in the depth of our darkness. And you can now be one of those people, especially if you read what was written in the first sixteen chapters.

Now, moving on...the best way I can help you answer the question of how to help us, is to let many parents weigh-in on the answer to this question. But let me warn you, one size does not fit all. (This is another reason you should read the other chapters of this book; to make sure you don't just go out and "do," without being aware of the height, depth, and width of the pain in our upside-down-turned-inside-out world.)

C.L.C.: Just be there for them and stay in touch. Many bereaved parents sadly lose friends after their loss. Which adds to the sadness. Stay in touch!

D.K.: A hug and I'm praying for you is all I need to hear. I'm blessed, because my friend sends my husband & I a text everyday of a verse from the bible, and my sister-in-loves text me often to say I love you and I'm praying for you. Just being here for my husband & I is a huge help.

D.T.: The best thing my friends can do is let me talk about my son. I love talking about him. He was just 17. I don't want to make my friends uncomfortable but it is the greatest gift they can give me.

K.D.: Sincerity is all I ask. When my son died, a couple of weeks later a friend asked me, "Is there anything I can do for you to help?" I said that I just haven't had the time to clean my car. I got a look of disbelief and a gaping mouth looking back at me with a, "What?" Don't say it if you don't mean it...

S.M.:..I would say that most people like to talk about their lost child, and as time goes by, they lose their audience as there is no "news" to share. If you see something that reminds you of their lost child, remark on it...if you see a movie, eat a favorite food, etc. just make a passing remark to let them know that you haven't forgotten their child. Perhaps ask if there is something you can do on "special" dates that will pose especially difficult for them - birthdays, anniversary of death, etc...most of us don't want to ask for help and try to go it alone even though help is needed.

S.M.: Certainly offer activities but don't force it. It's hard to go out and face people after losing a child, it's scary. Just be there to listen when they want to talk or just sit quietly. Stay in touch. Take them a meal or 2.

T.S.: Don't just tell them you're there for them. Show up on their doorstep maybe with a couple coffees or soda for each of you. I have very few visitors even after telling them that I will need you; but don't wait for me to ask because I won't be able to…If it wasn't for my neighbor coming down to just sit with me & watch TV at night or just talk, I don't know if I would have made it this far. Be there in person not just spirit.

T.J.: Please don't "talk" them into doing anything. Often it is the notes and cards in the mail that mean the most, the gift card for groceries, and if you offer to listen - then mean it. Just listen. Please don't "should" on bereaved parents. You should do this, you should do that.

S.R.: Sometimes I wish there was a book of etiquette to follow because people sincerely do not know how to help…A few things: Listen. Learn to listen to those grieving the loss of their child. Be there. You don't need eloquent words or memorized bible verses. Just be there with a hug. Mention the child's name. Believe me, the parents know their child's name and are thinking of their child 24/7. Be practical. Offer to run errands, cook a meal, or just sit with the one grieving. For a long, long time we're living in a "grief fog" and can't even remember how to get dressed!!!! And, lastly, even though your life has gone on, the life of those grieving the loss of child will never be the same. So, don't put pressure on by saying "We sure will be glad when you're your old self again!" That "old self" will never be the same again!

V.B.: What is extremely important is that friends must realize that this is a time they will be doing most of the work for the friendship. Friends must call, friends must send invitations, friends must be there for the grieving friend, always. A bereaved person will not have the capacity to reciprocate the friendship in *a way that you are used to. BUT be there anyway. Make those friendly phone calls. Ask 100 times over the next year if you can help, if you can do something. The bereaved person may not hear you the first 99 times, but that 100th time, they will be so grateful and will start to reciprocate when they are healthy and start living again.*

D.H.: *Bereaved parents are a prickly bunch, due to the trauma, grief, anger, PTSD, etc. I personally, am very prickly. But the friends who have stuck by me have been willing to walk with me in that dark place, if that's where I need to go sometimes. They talk about my son, speak his name, say how they miss him, too. And they ASK me what I need.*

C.D.: *I feel the most important thing is just to let them know that you are there for them no matter what they are feeling that day…unless they called me and talked, I would never call them at this time because my head and heart just aren't there. And please don't feel like you can't cry with them....it is comforting in a strange way when you know your friends hurt with you.*

K.C.: *…An amazing thing is when my friends or family randomly share a memory, or even better, if they remember an important date before I say anything. Just lets me know they miss him too, and still think about him. A quick text the day before an anniversary date or holiday is very special…Be with them and let them go through whatever they are going through at that moment, with no attempts to fix anything, because you just can't.*

J.B.A.: *For me, I appreciated phone calls and lunches or dinners with one or two people where there was a chance to talk about my daughter. Large groups or events that went on as if nothing had ever happened were just too hard.*

C.R.W.: *Just be there for them. Cook dinner for them, a card in the mail to let them know u care, maybe go over and clean for them. And don't be afraid to mention their child's name, it means more to us than u know to have our child's name brought up, it makes us feel good to know they are not being forgotten because all we can think about is our child.*

M.H.: When my daughter died twelve years ago, I found out I had one true friend; she came to my house every morning at 5 a.m. and stayed for hours, we drank pots of coffee, laughed, cried, talked and prayed! She did this for three months, some days she came back in the afternoon! If God had not sent her to me I don't know what I would have done!

L.V.B.: ...Do not dessert them as so many people do when they no longer know what to say. You might even ask them how you can most help them. Do they want you to talk about him, or does that cause more pain? And be prepared for that answer to change as time goes on.

P.W.: Yes ,yes ,yes mention the child's name! It just means she was real and alive and vital. You will not contribute to my grief by saying (daughter's) name, but you will be helping me in my grief.

L.S.: Although we had a lot of support online....It was a very lonely time... My husband's sister sent us a few little "in memory" gifts which was comforting...

S.L.: I lost 3 children in 2010 and my world almost fell apart... For 5 years I held on to guilt, anger, more guilt; and then a wonderful lady gave me time. She sat with me on the floor in my living room when she most certainly had other appointments to keep (I know because she rang her offices and cancelled them all) and let me take my memory boxes down from their shelf, both physical and emotional, and listened, and listened and cried with me and smiled with me but MOST importantly she let me talk. She didn't say one word until I had finished. No I understand, no how awful, just her presence when she knew it was my time to acknowledge my children, their lives, even though short, their deaths, and finally that I was their mother and nothing anyone said could change that. For me it was the turning point that I needed to off load everything so that I could celebrate my memories of them.

L.A.: "How are you doing?" DOES help so much! Not just 3 days or weeks later, but years later.

R.E.: ...The family is all so heartbroken we don't have an easy time being together as often... If only people would take two minutes to simply say, "I'm thinking of you today. I don't understand what you're going through exactly, but I know your heart is broken. Please know that I care." A small word of caring goes a long, long way in helping a person who is dealing with the pain of losing a child!

C.N.: ...You have to genuinely just be there. There will be days your friend will want to lay in bed and cry all day, let her! Lay with her! And there will be other days you need to pull her out of bed and get her moving. Encourage her to get into something for the day or get together somewhere with her. With us, we get together for the purpose of the other children.

P.P.: ... it has been 16 years for me...I tell friends to not say "call me if you need me" actually pick up the phone and call! Do not say "I can do whatever you need done," GO, be there and do what you see needs to be done. And do not let those you love that are suffering and grieving, do it alone. BE THERE. I try to tell them on all those special days, birthdays, mother's day, etc if you can't call because you "don't know what to say" well buy a card, write the child's name, let the parents know you remember!!!!!

So, did you catch the two main messages?
1. Let us know you care. Nothing big. Just a hug, a text, a card, come and be with us, do a simple day-to-day task for us... To us, the little things *are* the big things.
2. Remember my child with me. Over and over again the parents responded to this question by wanting to have someone to share their child with. We want to hear our child's name. We want to share stories. And if the tears flow, it is a needed cry, so please be okay with it and pass us the tissues.

For me personally, one of the things I absolutely love is when someone puts a post on my daughter's Facebook page! Sometimes someone will post an old picture they came across, or share something they know would make her laugh, or write in a memory they thought of, or just tell her they miss her. It is so very precious to me.

There is one last response from a pareavor I would like to share with you. She does a beautiful job of summing up the essence of how you can truly help us.

> *L.F.C.: In the early months, the simplest of daily chores can be overwhelming. I remember feeling frozen in every single way after (daughter) died and managing a shower was often my sole daily accomplishment. If someone asked what they could do, or tried to help me talk about my feelings - well, it was as if they were speaking a foreign language. I could see their mouths moving, even recognize the words they were speaking, yet it made no sense to me. I was too frozen, too numb, too far removed from my own life and body to make sense of what they said. Yet what stays with me now, almost ten years later, are the acts of kindness that were done without asking me what I needed, without requiring from me the effort of participation. The friend who quietly slipped into the house and ran a load of laundry or who vacuumed the floor, the home cooked meals left on my doorstep, the messages on my voice mail which said no need to call me back just want you to know I'm thinking of you, the flowers sent on holidays and her birthday that first year - these were lifelines of care and love that wordlessly, soundlessly, let me know there was a world waiting for me when I was ready to return to it. I will always be grateful for their willingness to give so thoughtfully and for their patience as they waited for me to come back.*

Thank you so very much for wanting to reach out and help us. We all hope you never have to find out personally how much it means to us.

Words of Grace and Hope

S.M.:... There is a world of love in the comfort of knowing there is a friend who just remains in my life even when I wouldn't want to be in my own life.

T.W.B.: A simple thing like a text message saying "I'm thinking of you" gives me so much comfort. It doesn't require much...just one friend reaching out to another friend.

P.M.: ... pray each day that God will nudge you at just the right time to just show an act of kindness or support in some way...

CHAPTER 18

||||||||||

Things to Avoid Saying to a Bereaved Parent

There are some people who just don't think before they speak, and say very hurtful things to a parent who is dealing with the death of their child. There are also some people who mean well, giving little cliché statements, which hurts as well.

This chapter is a "collage" of hurtful things said to pareavors which I have collected over time. Let me qualify this by letting you know the fresher the loss, the more important it is to avoid these careless comments. Some of them will be okay, further down the road when we begin to need the truth of the Word spoken into our lives. But for the first few weeks (and even months or years for some of us), these things can be like pouring salt into our raw, open and wounded hearts. We are very sensitive in our brokenness and can become hard and bitter if enough people say these hurtful things, making our healing that much more difficult.

If you want to find an actual list (without the colorful commentaries, aka sarcasm) of things not to say to a grieving parent (or anyone in mourning for that matter) to easily share with others, you can find one on our website at www.gpshope.org.

> G.G.: *A lot of things people say don't help. The worst for me to hear is "she is in a better place." I know this. But my heart is feeling what can be better than being here with me, her Mother and her 4 Beautiful Daughters??*

C.D.J.: Stay away from all the clichés and do not offer advice. The normal loss clichés do not apply to child loss and unless you've lost a child, you are not even remotely equipped to offer advice. And whatever you do, try not to get personally offended for anything they do or say. They are in pain you cannot imagine. They are completely devastated, confused, angry, sad, and the anxiety can be overwhelming. .

S.L.: Never tell them to move forward. Their world as they once knew it has been shattered, they will get through it in their own time and in their own way. It does NOT help a person who is grieving the loss of their child.

T.L.: A sentence not to say to a grieving Mother. "I didn't realize you were STILL struggling."

L.S.: I did get some rude insensitive comments..... I was told to move on just after a few weeks of my baby passing, I was told to see someone like I was crazy...I was told I'm not a mother anymore....I was told I could always have another one...but in fact it took us a year to conceive when we were ready to try, so it was not easy.

M: people told me to pretend (child) had gone to Australia....

P: someone said that I was lucky to have had (child) for 22 years. Would they have felt lucky if they had a limit on how long they would have their child?

One time I was reading a feed line on social media where someone had lost a sibling, and her mom was in the deepest part of the grieving process. This young lady was reaching out to other bereaved parents, describing her mom's total despondency, asking how she could help her mom. So many pareavors were saying things like "I was exactly where your mom is. Here is what helped me..." or "Just be with her. She has to work her own way out, and she will, eventually." Dozens of moms let her know that as difficult as it was to watch, this was normal after her loss.

Then someone had this answer on how to help her mom, "I have lost loved ones but not a child. It sounds like your mom is stuck in her grieving process and cannot move on. All her energy goes toward grieving. She absolutely needs counseling and medication. She is drowning and needs someone to pull her out of her despair. The sooner the better!" Wow! May I suggest if you haven't lost a child, and those who have experienced it are reaching out to help a pareavor, then please don't try to give them your solution that goes against what those who have experienced it are giving.

Another time, someone suggested helping a grieving mom by calling the police department and requesting a "welfare check" for an evaluation to see if she needed to be checked into the psychiatric ward of a hospital. This person said they will even come and get her and take her there, speaking from experience. There probably are a tiny handful of pareavors who need some sort of intervention, but if someone had called social services on me and had me hauled away for an evaluation to get the "help" I needed, it would have messed me up so bad I don't know if I would have ever been able to get past it! The thought of that actually makes me sick to my stomach.

There are several common statements we pareavors hear that people think will comfort us, Please allow me to share with you the ones that don't help, and can even cause us more pain and grief.

Don't tell us that God needed another angel. God doesn't kill children to fill some sort of angel roster. Plus, there is no support in the Bible that we turn into angels when we die. (Sorry to those who love "It's A Wonderful Life." It's a great classic with a good message, but Clarence didn't really earn his angel wings.)

Don't tell us how wonderful it is that we still have other children (or that we can just have more). Children are not interchangeable or replaceable. The loss of our child and the special relationship with that child cannot be replaced by another child. If my arm gets cut off, my ear isn't going to replace it or make up for it.

Please don't try to make us feel better by telling us our child is in a better place now. When someone told me that at the visitation, it took everything in me to not look absolutely shocked and exclaim, "REALLY??? Wow! I did not know that. Thank you for that news! Now I am all better and won't miss her anymore!" Good thing I had a friend with me to keep me in check. I *know* she is in a better place (I am actually much more aware of it than you are), but she was supposed to go there *after* me, not before me. Knowing where she is does not erase the intense pain of how wrong it is to have my child precede me in death, and to not have her here with us.

Don't tell us the lie that God doesn't give us more than we can handle. This is *not* a comforting statement. There are a lot of people who get more dumped on them than any one person should ever have to handle in this life. Plus, there is nothing in the Bible to support that statement. God says that we will not be tempted beyond what we are able to handle, and will always give us a way out (First Corinthians 10:13). If we are not "given" more than we can handle, how do you explain the rise in suicides in our young people? We live in a fallen, sinful, corrupt world, and we all pay the price from the crap (excuse my language) life hands us. In fact, Jesus warns us multiple times that our lives *will* have tribulation.

"It was God's will, even if we don't understand it." Unless you are God, don't use this line, especially to someone who is grieving the death of their child.

Here is a similar statement. "God must have a reason; you just need to trust Him." Unless the grieving parent is *very* rooted in the Lord and has already walked through some sort of previous tragedies in their lives, most parents are bitterly questioning why God allowed this death that makes no sense and is causing such intense pain. A statement like this can fuel the fire to be angry at God and blame Him, asking how God can be trusted when He allowed such a horrific event in our lives. This is something they will need to work out over time, but not have it thrown in their face, especially at the funeral or memorial service, or the first several weeks, or even months.

Please don't try to tell us your ideas of why it might have happened – how God is going to use it in the grand scheme of things - even when we ask "Why?" Let us know you don't have any answers either. At some point, our "why" has to turn to "How?" How am I going to get to the other side of this darkness? Let us know it is okay to be angry, even at God. (I address this in *When Tragedy Strikes*.) Let us know you agree that it's not okay our child is gone, and it doesn't make sense. It's okay to be shocked along with us, and not try to offer empty explanations.

"Remember, God promises to work everything out for our good" is another insensitive thing to say in the early stages (from my personal experience). We can't see the future through the thick black fog, and it adds to the frustration of what we are already dealing with. I was well aware of this verse, but at that point I was still shocked at what had happened, and I just wanted to wake up and have my child back!

"You are so strong. I could never go through what you are going through." We hope you never do, but you just might find yourself going through it someday! You don't get a choice in the matter. To tell us you could never face what we are facing makes it sound like we chose to lose our child; that we were not forced into this horrible nightmare. And please don't tell us how strong we are. What you see on the outside is nothing but a barely held together shell of our shattered interior. We are weak. Very, very weak, and exhausted, and confused, and in so much pain that some days all we can do is move from our bed to a chair, if even that.

Please respect our boundaries when we say we really don't want help with something, and don't take it personally or be offended. Often we feel like we have lost all control of our lives, and doing certain things helps us to counter that.

Do not tell a parent they need closure so they can move on. I have never heard of a parent getting closure.

Maybe they eventually found out the details of their child's death. But it didn't bring closure; not like other people might have with the death of a parent or spouse or someone else. As a parent, we never close that part of our life. It becomes something that molds us into a different person than we were before. There is no such thing as closure. It causes a change that keeps us from ever being the same.

Don't fall apart, sobbing on the shoulder of the grieving parent. A few tears of acknowledgment of my pain as someone talked to me at the visitation was actually comforting. But it drained so much energy to hold myself together to console people who were bawling on my shoulder about *their* loss when it was my daughter who had died! (And I don't mean those within the immediate family circle who can cry together, or a very close friend who is part of our inner circle.)

That leads me to an excellent article that I came across a couple of years after Becca died (by Susan Silk and Barry Goldman on the website of the LA Times). The article was about something called the Ring Theory: How Not to Say the Wrong Thing. It is getting to be more widely known, but this was the first time I heard about it.

When someone is in the hospital, there are those who want to go visit them. Depending on the circumstance and why the patient is there, the issue can either be too serious to have visitors, or the patient (or their families, or both) don't have the energy to have someone come and visit them. Believe it or not, this can actually cause people to be offended, when they are asked not to come.

This article said that when Susan had breast cancer, she had a colleague who wanted to visit her after a surgery. When Susan told this colleague she didn't want to have any visitors, the person's response was, "This isn't just about you." Very strange; how was Susan's cancer not about Susan?

We experienced this kind of thing ourselves. The last 18 months of her life, Becca spent well over half of her time an hour away in the Madison University Hospital, often in the cardiac ICU. When not in ICU, she was still kept in the transplant/cardiac unit, because she had very serious heart issues. When Becca wasn't in ICU, people thought they should be able to come and visit her. Sometimes she felt well (even quite lively) and other times she could be very ill. We lost a friend because of a time Becca only wanted to see family, and this friend thought she should be an exception. She has barely spoken to any of us since then.

Becca passed away the evening of October 12, 2011 in her hospital bed in that cardiac unit. The next morning, we went with our son-in-law to the funeral home to make all the decisions and arrangements no parent should ever have to make. Upon arriving back home, my mom was at the house. I had not seen her yet, and I just collapsed into her arms sobbing. As I did so, out of the corner of my eye, I saw two young ladies who had been in our church youth group, of which Becca had been a leader up to the time she became so ill. My daughter, who had just lost her sister, quickly hustled them into her bedroom, and became a hostess and comforter to these two girls who felt the need to come over to be with us as they were hurting the loss of Becca. Even though we loved these two young ladies and they were normally welcome in our home at any time, it was quite unnerving to me, to know people were in my home during this time of overwhelmingly intense pain that should have been for immediate family only.

So what do these things have to do with the Ring Theory?

Draw a circle. This is the center ring. The name of the person facing the trauma goes in that ring (such as the pareavor you want to help). Now draw a larger circle around the first one. In that ring put the name of the person next closest to the trauma (probably a spouse). Now draw another ring around that one. Put in the names of the people who come next in their closeness to that center person, such as children, their parents, maybe their siblings, or an extremely close best friend. Repeat the process as many times as you need to. In each larger ring put the next closest people.

The way it works is actually very simple. Comfort *in*, dump *out*.

In other words, the person in the center ring can say anything he or she wants to anyone, anywhere. She can complain, be angry, decide who she wants and doesn't want to see, ask "Why me?" and so on. She can dump on anyone at any time.

Everyone else can say those things too, but can only dump on people in larger rings. You cannot dump on someone who is in a ring smaller than the one you are in. Don't tell someone in a smaller ring how shocked you are at how bad the person looks who is dealing with the trauma. Don't tell them the situation is depressing you and bringing you down. Why not? Because they are closer to the person in crisis, and therefore carrying more of the heaviness of it, than you are. It is counterproductive, can be hurtful, and should not be added to what they are already dealing with. (And by the way, they also will not benefit from your advice.)

What we need is your comfort and support. Listening is often more helpful than talking. When you are talking to a person in a ring smaller than yours, someone closer to the center of the crisis, the goal is to help. Being supportive to the principal caregiver may be the best thing you can do for the patient. "I am praying for you and your family" is a comfort. "I am really hurting for you and so sorry you lost him" is a comfort. Giving a hug, giving time to help with something that needs to be done, letting us know you are praying for us, are all comforts.

If you want to cry or complain, tell someone how shocked or sad you are, or whine about how it reminds you of all the terrible things that have happened to you lately, make sure you do it to someone in an outer ring.

Most of us know enough not to dump into the center ring to the person dealing with the trauma. The Ring Theory just expands that intuition, and makes it more concrete: Don't just avoid dumping into the center ring, avoid dumping into any ring smaller than your own.

Remember, comfort *in*, dump *out*.

The bottom line is that no *person* can really give us the comfort we need. The pain is too deep, too intense. We desperately want to have our child back. Obviously, that is not going to happen. Eventually, the unkind things said to us don't hurt as much. We finally realize and come to grips with the fact that people don't mean to be stupid and hurtful with their words. They are saying what they think will help us. And in time (and by "time" I mean it can take several years), we discover that it doesn't have the same painful effect on us anymore... usually...

There is one thing I did not put on the list, because it deserves its own chapter. "I know how you feel because..."

Words of Grace and Hope

S.R.: There is always hope. God meets us in our grief. He suffers with us, comforts us, and sustains us.

D.D.P.: I always hated when people said God took our son or God needed another angel. The God I believe in doesn't do that to people. It was humanity that took our son, but I do believe God was there to receive him.

CHAPTER 19

||||||||||

I Know How You Feel Because...

Something I have noticed, is how *extremely* rare it is to hear a parent who has lost a child say to another pareavor, "I know how you feel." We know the pain is too individually deep to know how another parent feels. Each relationship between the child and the parent is so unique. I could never know how you feel, just like you could never know how I feel. Even if we lost a child in a similar way, such as a car accident, or the same form of cancer, we won't tell anyone who is grieving, "I know how you feel because..."

And yet, it is amazing how quickly someone who has never experienced the death of a child will tell us they know how we feel. "I know how you feel. I was devastated when my grandma died because we were really close." Or, "I know how you feel. I lost my husband several years ago and I thought I would never get over it" (said while holding on to the arm of her new husband). When a grieving parent is told something like this, the reaction it raises on the inside of us is oftentimes instant anger. We don't mean to feel that way. But to compare your loss with mine is so very, very wrong! I am sorry, but to tell me you know how it feels to bury my child because your aunt died and she practically raised you, just isn't the same thing. Painful and tragic? Yes, for sure! Does it feel the same as my pain? Sorry, but no.

And then there are those who tell us there are lots of things people lose; we all need to recover from the grief of our losses, and we get lumped into one big pot of grief. People need to use common sense when talking to pareavors.

Losing a job is *not* the same as the death of a child. Having a best friend move away is *not* the same as the death of a child. Losing money in investments is *not* the same as the death of a child. Losing a dog - no matter how old it was and how much that pet was loved - is *not* the same as the death of your own flesh-and-blood child. Do people need to work through the grief of these kinds of losses? Definitely! But don't try to tell me because you have suffered a painful loss that you know how it feels to have my child die, having part of my very being cut off from me.

I will use this opportunity to tell on myself. I *know* pets are part of our families. I *know* it can be very painful when they die. I *know* we have to grieve their loss. I have shed tears for several pets over the years (including my cat, Twinkles. I got her when in kindergarten and she didn't die until after my second child was born).

But I have never understood how anyone can elevate a pet to the status of a human being, even before the death of my daughter. Now that I have experienced that horrific pain, it is even harder for me to see how much sympathy is given to someone who loses a pet; or to discover when I google "grief support groups" that the loss of a pet comes up higher than the loss of someone to suicide! I feel like screaming, "WHAT IS WRONG WITH YOU PEOPLE!!!!"

While writing my book *When Tragedy Strikes* (coming out in bookstores July 5, 2016) there was a Facebook post that shocked and stunned me. For the most part, I do a pretty good job of keeping my mouth shut. (My family might not think so, but I really do, compared to the thoughts and emotions that are stirring inside of me.) But when I read this post, I just couldn't stay out of it. Let me allow me to share with you what was posted, my reply, and some of the things written as a result of my comment. I will admit…on second hand…I will admit nothing. I actually erased what I really wanted to write several times, to make sure what I wrote was very mild compared to what I was shouting on the inside.

> Post: *Tonight my heart is broken; our beloved family cat died after her second battle with cancer I feel like we lost a child.*

Fourteen people immediately offered their condolences and shared how sorry they were for her loss.

> My comment: *Okay I am NOT diminishing the fact that a beloved family pet can be very painful when it dies. But as someone who has lost a child, I can absolutely 500% guarantee you that losing a pet, no matter how much you loved it, is not even close to comparable to the pain of losing your actual child that you conceived, gave birth to and was a part of your very soul and being! I am sorry, but as a parent who is still grieving years later with easily flowing tears, I have a hard time when people compare losing their pets to losing a child...There is no word that even exists in the human language that can describe that kind of pain and the deep dark place it takes us. I pray you NEVER have to find out the true pain of burying your child. It changes who we are as a person... I am actually away for the week writing a book for grieving parents...so this is very heavy on my heart right now, even more than usual...I would gladly lose my 17 year old cat I love dearly any day if it meant I could get my Becca back...*
>
> Someone's comment to me: *I'm sorry for your loss... & agree with your comment... I'm just puzzled as to y u feel the need to trivialize (name) pain of losing her pet... she said nothing that warranted your attack... I hope you're getting help to deal with your grief...*

Okay, am I the only one who is trying not to picture myself reaching through the computer screen to do harm to someone on the other side? Where do I even start? It still makes my blood boil, reading it a year later! So do you think I just left it alone and went on my merry way? That would have been the "Christian" thing to do, I'm pretty sure, but I was definitely walking more in the pain of my soul than the peace of my spirit.

> My response: *(Name) I started out by saying I was NOT diminishing her pain, just saying while it is extremely painful to lose a pet that has been part of the family, to compare it to losing an actual child is...well, I said it already. I don't need help with dealing with my grief as you might think. That is another thing that only parents who have lost a child can understand. It is not something you ever get over. You learn how to function in a new way...I am sorry if it seemed I was attacking. Most grieving parents do it silently, isolated in their intense pain of loss for the rest of their lives for exactly these kinds of reasons. (To the person who posted) I am sorry if you felt "attacked". I am sorry you lost your cat. I know it hurts. We all need to grieve our losses...*
> Comment to me from a second person: *Actually losing a pet can be just as bad as losing a person in your life especially since (name of pet) has been in our lives for a long long time .she's not like any "pet" she was like a person .I agree with (name of first commenting person).*

Ok, I know there is absolutely no way someone who has not lost a child to death can know the deep dark pain and the black hole it puts us into. But we would at least like to know they are feeling some sort of empathy for us, and especially not insist that the loss of an animal can be as horrific as the death of our own flesh and blood child who is *supposed* to outlive us!

At that point I just found myself muttering "idiots!" and trying to put it out of my mind and get my peace back from being so agitated by the whole thing.

I will say the person who put up the original post eventually got on and wrote the following comment:

> *Laura, I would never ever think that losing a pet is more painful than losing a child. I never meant for it to come out like that. I could not even think about the pain you must have been*

through or are going through. I'm so sorry, I was just so heart broken and must have wrote it down wrong - please forgive me.

It is amazing how much of a healing balm something so simple like those few sentences can be to our shattered hearts and oozing pain. Instead of getting entangled in a conversation with the chance of feeling attacked again for voicing the painful truth, I simply gave it a thumbs up "like" and forced myself to let it go.

It isn't just me. This is a very painful subject for parents who have lost a child to death; to have another person say they know how it feels to lose a child because they lost... (and it has nothing to do with losing a child). Those who have lost both a child and a spouse, or a child and a parent, etc. will say the loss of their child has taken them to a place of much darker and intense pain, and that place of darkness and pain stays with them for way longer.

Here are a few thoughts from pareavors on this subject from behind the scenes.

M.D.G.: Some of the things people say to us during this time blows my mind. I have a family member who lost their job and it is all I hear when we do talk. Well I lost my son...hello! Better for me to be alone.
B.B.: We have lost a brother, father, pet of 10 years, many friends. Nothing, absolutely nothing is as horrendous as losing our 25 yo daughter ...We have some days where we seem ok. We have many days where uncontrolled emotions take over at even a happy life moment, movies, music or discussions...
A.W.T.: I love the folks that try to support and claim that they identify with my loss by comparing their loss of a grandmother or a father......not at all the same... unexplainable loss... no words for the pain ....no words...you can support and hold my hand while I share my memories and laugh with me, but do not compare.
M.P.: We lost our eldest at ten and her twin at twenty, people told me "you must find it easier having lost one, you'll be used

to it by now" Easy? Used to it? Never. My daughters are the only ones who have heard my heart beating from the inside and they have my heart, they always will, my heart broke with each loss. People just don't think how insensitive and hurtful they are with their comments and comparisons, losing your children is nothing like losing an elderly relative, it is not natural to outlive your children.

L.F.: I lost my mom and dad and my brother and sister and I thought that was heartache. It was nothing compared to the loss of my son and daughter, my son 2003 and my daughter 2011 both tragically. That is a heartache that cannot be described to anyone... it is a pain that no one can cure... it is a longing that never goes away... it is the emptiness you feel inside... it is the tears that never dry...

K.B.: What I have learned is a majority of people don't mean to hurt us by their words. They think they're helping, because they don't understand... Some will continue to say these things and some will just completely shut you out or barely talk to you because they don't know how to handle it or don't want to handle it... I've realized thru my journey my faith in God is the only one I can depend on 100% because even your closest friends and family relationships change during any kind of child loss.

A.H.: Unless someone has experienced the death of a human ...they carried and fostered hopes and dreams ... nurtured and helped the child grow, making mistakes, doing things wrong, trying to do better. Unless they felt the changes in the hugs and the blossoming of love, felt the pride of the child's accomplishments and watched them grow to be an adult, ... Unless someone has had all that end, suddenly with finality. Then they cannot identify with my loss. Only someone coping with that loss knows what I feel. Only they can say with truth I understand.

D.C.: We can't expect anyone else to "get it!" Without going through losing a child you can't understand. I can hardly understand it and I'm living it!

I Know How You Feel Because…

N.H.: *The hurt in my heart and the ache in my arms, can NOT be compared to any other loss at all.. The emptiness that is now and forever, my inner core, can NOT be compared to anything else at all..!!*

T.C.: *I tell my family and friends this all the time… I will never be the same!! Time will not heal this!! I use to say nothing when people compared it with the loss of a grandparent, but it bothered me so much!!! Now I just say very calmly, "let me know when you bury your child"… Even my own mother couldn't understand my pain!! My son is forever 18…*

S.H.R.: *I was just telling someone this the other day. I've lost grandparents, aunts, uncles, etc. There has been no loss that has compared to the loss of my daughter. The hole in my heart can't be fixed. There is no loss that can compare to this.*

B.L.: *I lost both of my parents, a brother and a sister, and as bad as I felt, THERE IS NO COMPARISON!!!!!!!!! The loss of my only child is the very worst thing that has ever happened to me and I feel the very deepest grief for mothers going through this agony!!!*

T.A.B.: *I have lost my mother, my father, my husband. Nothing compares to losing my son. All the pain is there and I miss each and every one of them, but my child had my heart and that hole will never be filled.*

M.M.: *too often I have coworkers compare their divorces, loss of their pet, or loss of their job, etc to the pain I'm feeling after losing my (son). Yes they have experienced loss but not to the magnitude of losing my child a piece of my heart!!! No comparison!!!*

H.K.S.: *Not having a husband is NOT the same as losing a child!!!!*

R.W.M.W.: *It's not the same losing a parent either. I lost my dad to cancer in 1989 and my son to a heart attack 3/4/2014.*

B.C.: *I hate it when people try to compare the loss of a pet to the loss of my child…it makes me want to choke them. (A kindred spirit LOL!)*

A.W.R.: *My favorite is when people say "I know how you feel, I lost my dog last year, he was like my child"...Seriously?! Did you carry him for almost 10 months; did you give birth to him? A pet is not a person!*

L.P.: *The worst thing that's ever been said to me is 'I know how you feel, or, I can imagine'. What a complete insult.*

C.D.J.: *Please know you are not alone. And even if it's 20 years or more since the loss, you are allowed to have those melt down days. Don't let anyone tell you otherwise. And if someone giving you advice has never lost a child, walk away... They don't have a clue. I get so sick of those who say, 'when I lost my mom, dad, aunt, great uncle, or my other favorite, dog' ... Ugh... just makes my blood boil.*

Please don't misunderstand. We know the death of any family member or friend can cause deep pain and trauma in a person's life. We are not minimizing other losses. All we are asking is for people to not compare losses, and to tell anyone who has experienced a devastating loss (especially someone who has lost a child through death), "I know how you feel because..."

Words of Grace and Hope

D.C.: *...I don't know how people without faith do this...God was with me from the very moment I got the news. Friends and family are great but they are human and will disappoint where God never will.*

D.B.: *We fight so many different emotions on a daily basis, and it's hard!! I give myself pep talks, and of course-I talk to God. I know that He is and always will be here for me, and I thank Him daily. I give Him the credit for carrying me when I just didn't feel as if I could even stand up! I believe in Heaven, and I know my beautiful children and husband are there, and I will see them again one day!*

CHAPTER 20

||||||||||

Please Don't Forget Us

As I have already stated, life goes back to normal very quickly for those around us. The funeral is over, a few days go by, and everyone else is moving forward with their lives as though nothing happened. We can't fault them for that...but it is hard to describe how we feel when our world has come crashing down around us, and just thinking about getting out of bed for the day can seem to sap us of all energy, much less getting dressed and doing anything considered part of day-to-day life.

The compassion and concern briefly offered by others comes to an end, and we are left drowning in a sea of grief, not knowing where to go with it for help or support. Not only do we feel alone and forgotten, but even more painful is feeling like our child has been forgotten.

If only those around us knew how much it means to have the life of our child remembered! A card in the mail, a hug, a quick phone call (even if we don't answer and you leave a message) means so much to us. We were thrown into dark and terrifying waters, and ongoing support is a life-line we so desperately need.

> H.J.: *I'm afraid he'll be forgotten by friends and family...our (son) was braver than anyone I knew.....he left us on Feb 28th 2014, I'm the only one who posts to his Facebook page...it's sad, but I think he's already been forgotten...breaks my heart because he's so unforgettable. My heart aches each and every day with missing my (son).*
> C.L.: *4 years yesterday since our beloved 17 year old son was taken home. I was just saying today that people don't*

understand the importance of remembering them. It's okay to make us cry; it's okay to say their names, we want that. Don't ignore us or the fact that we have lost our child; that just hurts worse.

C.C.F.: Yes my friends have floated away since my daughter died 6 years ago. I literally just have my husband and son. Very lonely. I don't talk a lot.

K.C.: I bring my son (name) up almost daily. I can tell by the look on people's faces they don't know how to react. All I want is to keep his memory alive. In the end memories are all we have.

K.R.: My daughter passed Jan. 19, 2014 and there isn't a day that passes that I don't think of her - I agree people move around as if it's a normal day and don't understand the pain that a parent goes through and the emptiness you feel.

A.H.: ...I feel like no one even gives us a thought anymore...

C.S.: ...everyone forgets and you are left alone to deal with the daily heart crushing pain...

B.M.G.: Love when people bring up my sons name! It lets me know they miss him too

A.D.: My beautiful (son) has been gone for more than 26 months. I loved him for more than 20 years & I still cry almost every day. Most of my friends and family have distanced themselves. It's a really lonely place and I imagine it always will be. I'm very grateful for the small handful of people who have stuck by my side.

D.S.W.: Sadly I don't think it will ever change but this is just so so true; just a simple call or hug or mention of his name so one knows he meant something to them.

C.M.: I have never felt so alone in my life!!...

J.B.: In the beginning I wanted everyone to remember my son. I soon found out it didn't matter since I was his mother and had him in my heart forever. That's all that matters to me now.

T.T.: After almost 29 years of my beautiful daughter (name) being gone I still LOVE when someone mentions her name.

C.G.:...People tell you they are sorry and sign a card and give it to you and then it's over for them ....unknowingly that it will never be over for us and we have a big gaping hole in our hearts that can never be fixed. That our lives are forever changed in a way they will never know (hopefully). I do want people to remember (daughter) but just a few will and eventually no one will. I will honor my precious daughter every day for the rest of my life.

M.B.R.: It's been 9 months. Not a day goes by that I don't still ache with grief. He would have been 20 next month and I cannot fathom how hard that day will be. I still LOVE walking into his room and taking in that over powering stinky teenage boy smell. I used to hate it but now I can't get enough.

J.C.G.: People don't realize this is a LIFE LONG journey for us!

J.B.C.: Everyone has forgotten my son ever existed. No one says his name or shares a memory. It feels like there is a knife in my chest.

S.S.: ...it's been 7 months since (son) passed. Nobody asks how I really am... If we've got on our "outside" face they don't mention your child's name, cause it looks like we're ok.

A.S.: I have a friend that has never left my side. From the time the police knocked on my door till today I see her. She checks up on me I simply call her my walking, talking Angel. Without her I wouldn't be here & I lost my entire family Husband, daughter & son on 12/12/02 I will forever be grateful for my Friend looking after me she is truly amazing. She is my sun on a cloudy day.

J.L.: ...It's always nice to hear from others who remember (daughter) used to do this or say that. It makes me feel good for a moment. On the other hand it hurts so much to see others with their kids. I feel so lost and crazy with all of these so contradicting feelings.

R.E.: I lost 2 grown children and a teenage granddaughter in less than 5 years. My large group of friends has dropped to 3 who I can trust...people treat me like my "bad luck" will rub off on them.

A.M.H.: It doesn't end in a year or two or TEN. We understand how others that haven't been affected by our loss can

131

> *move on...WHY can't they understand that we have been DEEPLY affected by our loss and that we will never be able to live life as we used to?*
> **L.T.:** *I lost my son 8 years ago and still hurt as much as I did on the day he died, possibly hurt more. Yes I smile and try to get on with my life but my heart is totally broken and will be forever. I still cry for him every day. Friends have come & gone and it is a very rare event when I am asked "how are you."*
> **P.M.:** *Every time I mentioned (son's) name people would stop talking and look around and be uncomfortable. Till one day I was talking to my sister about old times and I brought up his name and she just stopped and stared. And this is what I said, "He was my son he walked this earth, I will remember him every day and I will talk about him; he was and is part of my life." Well things changed... My son died before Facebook. My sister got with relatives and started sharing pictures of the family, both old ones new ones and they tagged (son) in every one he was in, made my heart jump for joy...*

As you have read, this doesn't just go away after a year, or two, or six. There are times we get thrown back into that pit of grief and despair, not because we want to, but because something triggered the painful remembrance of our loss. Many people only want their lives to be filled with happy thoughts and so they drift away from us, so as not to be around us downers.

I understand life gets busy, and there are many of our family and friends with good intentions. But if you would please stop and think about how your life would instantly change, if one of your children were taken from you through death. Would you want the people who are involved in your life to be there for you in your darkest days?

Please, oh please, be there for us.

Words of Grace and Hope

> **D.H.L.:** *I lost my son at 20. The only reason I allowed joy back into my life was because his precious friends came to visit*

and implored me not to be so sad and lost. They told me that they knew my (son) so well and that he would be devastated if he knew how much I was suffering. That he would want me to go on and have joy in my life. That was my defining moment that I chose to still find joy. Don't get me wrong, it's still a challenge 14 years later, but each time I "relapse" I think of that day the boys came by to see me. I thank God for those boys!

A.I.C.N.: I lost my youngest daughter, (name) five years ago. I miss her so. It helps me to remember a vision I had of her telling me she is happiest when I am happy. It gives me permission to experience love and joy and peace and filling of the Holy Spirit. It helps me so much to also to think of needing to stay strong for my two older children.

CHAPTER 21

|||||||||||

Words of Hope from Bereaved Parents

Hope. Without it, we can't move forward. That is true of anyone, but especially for pareavors. Unfortunately, we have been dealt such a huge blow, and we often don't believe hope is ever possible. And when that belief of hope starts to become a glimmer of possibility, it can be a long time down the road. Not just a few months, but a few years.

I recently found out one of my classmates lost his son – three years before we lost Becca. At the six year mark, he was finally ready to put up a tombstone at the gravesite. I know several parents who had their child cremated, and years later the urn of ashes still has a prominent place in their home, as they are still not ready to part with their child. I have even heard of some parents who take their child's ashes on vacation with them.

Yes, I know, this doesn't sound like it is giving hope, does it? I just want you to be aware that hope for a grieving parent can be a long time in coming. And hope definitely isn't something that can be forced onto another person. It is easy for someone on the outside looking in to be able to see hope in someone else's future. But often when you are the one on the inside, trying to dig yourself out of a black pit you were hurled into, hope is almost impossible to see, much less believe in.

The best way for a grieving parent to find that hope they so desperately need is to hear from other parents who have been where they are, who can offer a hand of hope to them from their own experience.

So here we go.

K.S.R.: *When (husband) and I lost our son, it was the hope we had in the Lord to get us past the tears and into a place that we could go on living.*

K.C.: *I lost my 8 year old daughter 16 years ago this April in a car accident... the pain was indescribable. Without Christ in my life, I know I never could have gotten to the place where I am today. It's still painful but I have peace & have shared in many churches & youth conferences my testimony of the healing power of God.*

P.G.B.: *That hole remains forever more, yet I believe it can heal. Without that belief, it leaves us hopeless... My hope remains in heaven when we will be reunited! I have two earthly children, a husband, two grandchildren and countless other family members and friends. We must pray for healing in our hearts for those relationships that remain. We live.*

R.W.: *I have lost 5 babies and have none today. My husband and I can tell you from personal experience, after 30 year of marriage that you never do get "over" the pain of losing your baby/babies, but God gives you comfort. For many reasons, people have a tendency to "put others down" for their tears. This is God's way of healing our hearts and giving us the venting of the pressure built up inside us.*

T.H.H.: *I lost my 5 year old son almost 17 years ago and I say now that if anyone could have got in my head back then, they would have thought I was crazy cause all the things I felt and thought..thankful to God that he has helped me.. Pain is still there and my heart has a hole in it but i know I'll see him again one day!!*

T.D.W.: *Myself I got into Christian music. Play it all the time. Turn it over to God and he will lead you through it. It will never go away but God is there... It took me 4 yrs. to function, laugh without guilt, finding a peace in my heart. It has been 6 yrs. and of course I have my days...*

T.P.R.: *My daughter has been gone 38 years and my son 2 3/4 yrs. I have one son living. Things will seem better, then out* of the blue I will be crying and the pain is fresh all over again... God alone has pulled me through this and I depend on him daily.

S.S.: There is nothing that will take the heartbreak away; the only thing that gets me through each day is our Lord Jesus Christ and reading his word...

S.C.D.: ...The pain never goes away.... I also have four other children, one who is not quite 15 and I have three grandchildren, one of which was (son's) daughter. No way am I giving up on my children and grandchildren by allowing grief to consume me to the point that I can't function.

G.U.O.: It's ok to miss your child. I miss my son (name) with every single breath I take. My heart is forever broken. But I am learning to smile again and celebrate his life. I thank God for the privilege of being his mom. But I also know my three other sons also deserve a happy life and a mom who loves them and can smile laugh and live. I thank God for that. It's been a journey and one I wouldn't wish on anyone. I miss my beautiful son; 18 years was just not enough.

J.O.: ... It has taken me a while, grief is the hardest thing I have ever done, but I refused, after I heard a young girl who had lost her sister say, "the day my sister died, my mom died too, she is just still breathing!...

L.S.: ...It has now been 11 years since my daughter's death, and there are still days that are emotional and longing for her, but with time you will laugh again and the joy will return. Those of us who believe and trust in Jesus all have HOPE that we will see our precious children again.

C.E.P.: I lost my 22 year old son 6 1/2 years ago. I choose not to live in the darkness of grief every day. I have two other children, two grandchildren, other family, a job, and a life that my son would want me to continue to live. I still have my days.... And I would not consider myself a normal grieving parent if I didn't.... I cry, scream. Miss my son desperately..... But I put my feet on the floor every day and find one good thing in each new day to be thankful for. It is up to you. We are all different in our grief. Find your path.... Walk it....

> M.E.T.: *The greatest gift I can give my son now that he went home to JESUS is to live for him!*

In reading what these parents have to say, there are two things you might have observed. First, almost every single one of them acknowledge their hope comes from God, who is the giver of all hope.

Second, this seems to be one of the shortest chapters in this book. That is because there are fewer pareavors offering hope than there are pareavors still fighting the gross darkness that comes with the death of a child; thus the need for those who can guide them in the direction of hope.

Dr. Norman H. Wright is one of those pareavors offering hope to those on the path behind him. Here is something he has to say to them, which is also good for our friends and family to know. "It's okay if you don't feel like there's any hope at this time. Coming up, there will be that day where that little glimmer of hope begins to weave its way into your life and then it begins to grow and to expand."

Here is some great advice to friends and family from a bereaved parent.

> T.K.M.: *I lost my youngest son 6 years ago; the message I would give you is this, remember the person, call once a month just to say hello and ask if you can pray with them or just talk. Send a card to uplift them. Believe me when I tell you that no matter what you do will probably make them cry, but that is ok, that is how we heal our hearts and souls. But the important thing is do not ignore them, confront their pain and share with them, let them know you love them. That is how I was able to get peace and feel loved, pass it on.*

Hope. It is something we all need. No one can truly live without it. Pray for us to have hope, and be there with us until we do.

Words of Grace and Hope

A.T.: Grief is real and it's a process. We have lost 2 children. Our oldest son 8 yrs ago and oldest daughter this past July. We don't understand why but I am here to tell you that there is a PEACE that you can have. Allow yourself to grieve and also allow yourself to smile laugh and feel joy. I think we even feel guilty at times for feeling joy after such horrible loss. I don't know how to explain it other than just fall in the lap of GOD and let him heal you. The old saying that time heals is a lie. Time does nothing but GOD lost HIS SON. JESUS WENT THRU SUCH HORRIBLE TORTURE AND DEATH. And it was for us so in times like this we can be reassured that we can be with our children again and we won't be separated ever again. Tears yes Sadness yes overwhelming heartache yes but this isn't forever. Only for a season. The Bible teaches. "TO BE ABSENT FROM THE BODY IS BEING PRESENT WITH THE LORD". I have to focus on the future when we will all be together again. I picture my children and they have gone on a trip ahead of us but we will be joining them. I PRAY THE LORD gives you the PEACE that is unexplainable.

CHAPTER 22

|||||||||

The Joy of Thinking About Seeing Them Again

Knowing I will see my daughter again when I leave this earth gives me a totally different perspective of death. I am especially blessed to have an actual document signed by all five of my children, making a commitment to "B-There." It was from a Focus on the Family event we went to many years ago. Both my husband and I consider it to be one of the most precious possessions we have, especially since we have a child who is already there in heaven waiting for us. (The words to this document are printed in *When Tragedy Strikes* by permission of Focus on the Family.)

At first, the thought of getting further and further away from Becca could put me in a tailspin. But one day, God graciously reminded me I was not getting further away from her, but closer to her. It is all in perspective. If I am thinking of my earthly loss, it is difficult, and her life gets further away from me. If I am thinking of my eternal home, the truth is that every day I am getting closer to seeing her again. I will readily admit it isn't always easy to make this shift in my thoughts. I still want her here with me now, and it hurts that she isn't here with us. As parents, we are supposed to leave this earth before our children. But thankfully this world is not our permanent home, and one day we will be together, never to be separated again.

So what about those parents who don't have the peace of knowing if their child accepted the gift of salvation? They can be in constant turmoil with this burden. Here are my personal thoughts on the subject.

> *God's love for your child supersedes your love for him or her. Each one of us is created with His desire to have an intimate relationship with us, not just here on earth, but for all of eternity. I believe God is big enough to have made every opportunity possible for your child to accept Him before leaving this earth. This could easily have happened during a time you know nothing about (including crying out to Him at the moment of death). So give that fear to God, trusting that He took care of it. Not having the information you want to have doesn't mean it did not happen at some point in their lives. (Taken from* When Tragedy Strikes.*)*

If you want to know for sure where you are going after your own death, you can *know* you will be in heaven, if you accept what Jesus did for you. Pareavors might be afraid to do this for fear of not knowing where their child is spending eternity, but I assure you, this is the best chance we all have of being together after this life.

God is such a gracious and loving Father, and He is clear that He gives everyone an opportunity to receive the gift of salvation. A child can receive the gift of salvation by being introduced to Jesus through a friend, and never tell their parents, thinking no one in the family would understand the decision he or she made that affected their eternal home.

And not only does accepting what Jesus did for us greatly increase a pareavor's chance of spending eternity with their child, but it opens the door for them to live a life with hope and purpose until they are together again.

If you, the reader, don't know God in this way, you can if you want to. He has been waiting for you; His heart is breaking for you, wanting to comfort you, bring you stillness and peace that cannot be explained or understood, and to just love on you in a way you have never known or been able to even imagine. Open yourself up to Him by telling Him you want and need Him in your life. Let Him know you believe and accept the price Jesus paid for your sin, which was to die

The Joy of Thinking About Seeing Them Again

as a sacrifice in your place. Ask Him to forgive you of your sins and to come live inside of you. Tell Him you are putting Him in charge of your life and surrendering to His ways, believing that as your Creator He has a special plan for your life.

If you are not familiar with the Bible, or don't know where to access more information to help you grow in this new life with God inside you, please go to our Crown of Glory website (www.crownofgloryministries.org) and register for our free members library, where you will find things to read, and resources to help you walk this new path you are on. You will also start receiving emails that will teach and encourage you on a regular basis.

It will be important for you to find a place where other believers in Christ get together on a regular basis, people you can spend time with who will help you grow and get stronger in your life with Him. God already has a place picked out for you, so be sure to ask Him to lead you to that place.

You can also share this information with the pareavors in your life. They might not be open to it at first, but just continue to be there for them, keep praying for them, and continue to gently offer God's loving and wonderful gift of heaven after this life on earth as the conversation and the Holy Spirit leads.

For those of us who know without a doubt our children are safe with the Lord, you will still find that even though we grieve with hope, we still grieve.

D.S.S.: I was just thinking about the loss of my son (name) from a little over 7 years ago. I know some people don't understand the grief I still have after what is considered all this time... I watched him become a young man. Then to lose him before he even hit his 30th birthday. We have been there from the moment our babies were conceived to the moment we lost that child. We won't have the honor of watching them grow older or to see what else life could have held for them. They're in

143

God's hands now and we can't call them, go out to eat with them, we can't do anything with them. Our world has been shaken to the core and yet we go on and go about our daily lives and love the ones we still have with us. I am thankful that my son is with God now and is living a glorious life every day in heaven.

Let's hear from more pareavors who are looking forward to that glorious day of being reunited with their children in heaven.

L.G.: I think about this every day. Just imagine that wonderful feeling we will have. It's a day of anticipation.
J.C.L.: I CAN ONLY IMAGINE...totally new heartfelt emotions from that song now!
T.I.C.: Each day that passes brings me one day closer to seeing my little (daughter) again, next time there will be no more goodbyes! My mom and my daughter are the reason I am not afraid of death, I look forward to seeing them both again!!
L.H.: That is the only thing that keeps me going! Miss my son so much even after 41 years! These feelings will never go until that day I'm back with my son (name)!
L.D.: ...Without my spiritual beliefs, which I also instilled in my precious daughter at a very young age, I would not have survived this. Without this spirituality, my daughter would have not have been able to face or go through the last few years of her life, with the strength and grace that she showed to me and others. The talks we had, when she had accepted her fate...... She was my only child. My body yearns for her every day. My comforts are that she no longer suffers, and I will be with her again...
D.W.C.: No more pain or tears or death when we see our kids again. HEAVEN!
B.S.: I never knew how much faith I had until I lost my son. I used to fear death but now I know I will get to be with my son & I don't fear it anymore.

The Joy of Thinking About Seeing Them Again

J.C.L.: ...I was so scared of dying even though I'm saved and know where I'll go. But not anymore...I'm ready anytime to be with my (child) again

J.I.R.: I think about that day every day, to be rejoined with my son (name). Every day is a day closer that I can hold my son again!!!!

L.D.: I think people feel uncomfortable and disturbed that we are giving up or wasting our lives thinking about being one day closer to our child! The fact is we will always have an empty place in our hearts and a desperate longing to see and hold them once more! That said, it does not mean we are not living, but living with a missing piece of our heart. If you have never lost a child it is very difficult for people even close to you to understand the depth of your pain...

R.H.: ...Looking forward to seeing her one day in Heaven gives me the strength to endure this difficult journey of losing her.

B.M.: ...I no longer fear death either. Each day means one day closer to being with my son again. People can't fully comprehend this, especially when you have other children. It's hard for people to understand that when your child left, so did part of your heart. I love all of my children and would do anything for them. But I don't feel bad about yearning to be in Heaven with my son... It's very conflicting feelings and your heart is constantly torn between life and the longing for being with your child in Heaven.

R.A.B.: I feel the exact same way, torn between 2 worlds, my living son needs me here, but I long to be with my other sons on the others side, I'm exhausted!!

P.T.: Without the hope of heaven and God's promises, I cannot imagine. His hope carries me through each day.

L.R.C.: It will be a great reunion in Heaven, miss my son so much! Thankful that I will see him again one day! It is a daily struggle, but my hope is in God .....

A.S.: Yes can't wait for that day to hug and kiss my baby girl again!!!

S.B.: *That thought keeps me getting up every morning; that Grand Reunion when I can hug my girl and tell her how much I love and miss her*

B.T.: *...We so look forward to that reunion with our child in heaven*

D.S.: *Such mixed feelings because I so want to see my son again in heaven but I don't want to leave my two children who are here. !!! But when the time comes I will know it's meant to be.*

K.T.: *My 15yr daughter asked me last night if I wished I could die to be with her brother. Even though sometimes I wish I could, I said no, I have you*

K.C.: *Your post made me start humming the hymn, When We All Get To HEAVEN. "What a day of rejoicing that will be!"*

M.C.: *The promise of heaven is the only thing that keeps me going.*

T.N.K.: *I cannot fathom living one day after (son's) death without the Hope and Faith of being with him again in paradise. Without God, I wouldn't be here today and that is the truth!!!*

N.L.: *I know heaven is real, my Jesus is real also, and I will see my son again with Jesus by my side in Heaven*

S.H.C.: *I know that a great reunion will be in heaven for me and my precious son. I also know that Jesus will be there to witness this wonderful reunion when it happens.*

J.B.: *The promise of seeing my baby in heaven is the only thing keeping me going. Without that belief how could any parent survive?*

D.H.: *The promise of Heaven and seeing my Son again is what I hang on to each and every day. I love all 5 of my children, there are 4 here on earth. I know God has a better plan than we can understand but missing my son is the hardest thing I have ever endured.*

G.R.: *I am so looking forward to the day I am reunited with my daughter, some days I feel like it can't get here soon enough. Life sucks, I am drained of everything. Physically and mentally.*

S.J.D.: Our oldest daughter died too soon...Our faith is what has brought us out of the darkness and back to God - without faith - there isn't anything.

M.C.R.: I ask every day how my son whom I was always so close to got so far away so fast. I know he is in heaven I can still feel his presence but I miss all of the physical things. His smile, his laugh, his beautiful green eyes and most of all I miss the kind of hugs I could only get from him. I hang on to the knowledge that we will be together again!

C.H.: Some days all we can think about is meeting our child again in heaven. We cling to that hope -- daydreaming about what that wonderful reunion is going to be like!!! And, I think that we can't even begin to imagine how wonderful it's going to be!!!

At the one year mark of Becca's death, I was with a friend who took me out for coffee and just let me share my heart and cry about Becca. One thing I shared with her is how horrible I felt that I was looking forward to going to heaven to see my daughter more than to see Jesus. Her response? "But, Laura, you've made a deposit!"

And that, my friends, is a perfect example of how to be there for us in the mixed emotions we have about wanting to be here and there at the same time!

Words of Grace and Hope

A.S.R.: What a day of rejoicing that will be.

S.B.: It's been 30 years since (son) left and 15 since (second son) joined him; each morning before getting out of bed and each night as I retire I tell my two boys in heaven that they better warn God when it's my time to arrive that heaven will not be the same cause my boys and I are gunna party hearty. I know they won't be the same as they were here, but love crosses all divides and a mother's love will know her children so watch out God, my earthly days are numbered and my party days are near!

CHAPTER 23

|||||||||

Choosing to Live Again

The reason I have become passionate about extending hope to pareavors is because there is so much out there from grieving parents who are stuck in their grief, telling other grieving parents their lives will never be the same; that it will always be dark, and life will never be worth living again without their child.

I personally refused to believe that.

I know that my life will never be the same, but I could not come into agreement that it would always be dark and not worth living. I have four other children and grandchildren. I have a calling on my life and an international ministry. I have the Seed of Hope and Life living inside of me. As horrific as it was, I did not believe the death of my child was where God reached His limit, and He was unable to help me work through it in triumph to a victorious life.

However, after saying all of that, it is extremely traumatic, and it does take months and years to work through the painful loss of our child being amputated from us, and start to see light in our darkness. It is a choice, and yet it isn't. Only those who have faced this blackness will truly understand what I am trying to put into words. There are those who choose to fight their way out, and those who don't. There are those who choose to die emotionally, and those who choose to find a way to live. And those of us who make the choices to fight and to live, do so at different times in our journey.

Here is a pareavor voicing this same issue I had when Becca left this earth.

> *We lost our wonderful 20-year-old daughter in a tragic car accident. I know and accept the fact that I will never get over the loss... from reading these posts, it seems like the rest of my life will be doom and gloom. It is bad enough that I lost the most precious thing in life and from reading most of these posts it seems like now we will be subjected to a life of grief and sorrow, void of any joy and hope. I want desperately to get some kind of a life back. We were a happy and fulfilled family before; we also have a 26-year-old daughter. Our home was full of love and laughter, now every day is dark and sad. I know it is early in our grief journey but the thought of living every day without smiling, light heartedness and some semblance of joy is terrifying. Nothing we will do will bring our beautiful daughter back; isn't that enough pain to endure; I mean why be alive, if this is all we have to look forward to?*

The following pareavors have chosen to fight, and to live their lives in as much joy and fullness as possible without their child by their side here on earth. They are doing their best to encourage those who can only find negative words of doom and gloom, that they can also choose to fight through the darkness to get back into the light of life.

> *L.T.H.: JOY was something I thought would never be in my life again after my 19 year old daughter died 14 years ago, I struggled for 10 years ... then one day I made the decision to finally start moving forward... I bought stocking hangers that spelled out JOY, a friend gave me a coffee cup that had the word JOY on it, it seemed the word JOY was everywhere I looked... What I did not realize was that JOY was all around me, I saw it in my son, I saw it in my work, and finally I saw it in myself. Joy is hard to achieve, you have to work at being happy, JOY is harder than grief... don't wait 10 years cause now I sometimes think I wasted some of those years but for me it took me that long . My son got married 2 years ago and they needed Christmas decorations so I went thru mine and I gave*

them my JOY stocking hangers ... I had to laugh at myself and said I'm giving away my JOY!!!!...

S.R.D.: *I am a mom who lost 3 little girls and my husband in a tragic house fire, (ages: 9 months, 4 and 8). I just had my 34th Angel day (Feb.1,1981)... my life did finally go on and I did smile again and was happy, but it took a lot of hard work for me to do this. I realize everyone isn't alike in this thing we call "Grief", but for myself I did go on....*

N.W.: *I went to a meeting after our son died 32 years ago at the age of 5. After a while I quit going because I felt like I was living the tragedy every day 2 years after his death... I do not do 4th of July and all my children know why. They never knew their oldest brother but they miss him just the same. They know when mom has her (name) days. My greatest joy is my grandson... Life does go on and you can choose to live in darkness or honor your child and live life as you think he or she would want you to.*

K.B.C.: *Our son was 23 when he had his accident almost 3 years ago... I dove straight into grief and now I am so thankful I did. It's hard work. I read books on grief the first year till my eyes couldn't read any more. I go to support meetings each week still. We are a very close family and strong in our faith. We laugh now, make vacation plans and live weeks without crying our eyes out...*

V.L.H.: *I think that basically the choice is yours. You can't change what happened; all you can change is how you let it affect you. I am very saddened to read messages from people who, years on, seem to be unable to find a glimpse of hope in their life without their child. But I don't think this need be the case. I lost my son 10 months ago to suicide and I miss him terribly, but I'm also able to enjoy my two other kids and my granddaughter and the company of my friends, and I can laugh and have fun. At the beginning I felt guilty about enjoying myself, but...why not? (I have to say that I have always been a positive, cheerful person, which no doubt helps). I owe it to myself, the rest of my family and to my beloved son to carry on ahead. I hope this doesn't sound insensitive, but it is a choice I* have made. Life goes on and I want to be as happy as I can be under the circumstances. Life will never be the same again, but it goes on...................

V.B.: ...I lost my oldest son. The first 6 months were horrible. I too read some posts and thought 10 years from now I'll feel the same way? I have 4 younger children and I didn't want their lives to be sad and without joy. So I started looking in other directions for grief guidance...They deserve the fun filled childhood my oldest had. It's not easy and requires thought but it's slowly happening.

T.L.W.: ...I remember feeling guilty the first day I didn't feel crushing heartbreak. But then I remembered that my daughter was laughter and life and light. I began to find ways to fill my days with those. After 11 years, there are doom and gloom moments, showers filled with tears, weird dreams, and the heart stopping moments when I see something she would have liked. But they are no longer the majority. Bittersweet bits of grief.

P.L.S.: ...it has been 9 yrs since my oldest son passed in a wreck, and today I laugh again. You will laugh again, you will smile again, you will feel joy again, and especially if you have other children to still love, hold and hear them call you mom... it's a very black journey for most of us, but we do get thru it. It's different for everyone, we all react differently to things, but this is one thing the most of us moms agree on, we could not have gotten thru it without each other's help and shoulders to cry on; the wisdom of the mothers who had gone thru it before us. I couldn't have made it without the groups, but I will say, once I was beyond the newness and had come out on the other side a totally different person, I had to pull away from the groups for a bit.

It seemed I would get back in the darkness really fast when I was reading post from parents who had just lost their child, so many new ones every day. I would cry so hard while trying to read and answer their questions, it started getting to me really bad. So I quit going to groups for a bit. I still today have to take breaks from it, but life goes on. We continue to breathe and I have lost 3 children to death too soon. But life stops for

> no one. It's our personal choice as to how much of our "normal" life we go back to.
> S.W.: The rest of your life will NOT be doom and gloom...only if you choose that. You can choose JOY. Our son passed away nearly 5 years ago and yes we do miss him every day. But we determined that we would choose joy, happiness, peace, laughter, etc. because he would never have wanted us to live life in doom and gloom. With God's help, we have been able to choose JOY and he can help you too. Today I Choose.....you have the choice...

When we do choose life and joy, it is hard work. It is a battle. It can be exhausting. But it can be done, and it is so very worth it!

And please understand when I say even though it is a choice we have to make, we cannot be pushed into making it. And of course as you have seen by now, each one of our paths is so very unique. There is no way "one size fits all" in this journey of losing a child.

So I ask you to pray. Pray for the one you care for to be connected to others on the path ahead of them who can be a light in their darkness. Pray for them to desire to see hope. And especially pray for them to choose life, and to have the strength and endurance needed to fight the greatest battle of their life to get it.

Words of Grace and Hope

> C.H.: YOU determine what your future will be! I lost my son 17 months ago and I live a very joyful life.
> S.W.: ...She has been gone now for longer than she lived. My life has not stood still; my grief did not hold its shape like concrete. It is a process through which we move, and we return to joy of a different kind, laced with gratitude for what we've had and what we still have... Choose to heal, and you will. Intend it! Then follow the path, step by step, until you're there.

CHAPTER 24

||||||||||

What Do I Do Now With This Information?

So here we are. Is your head spinning and your heart heavy from all the things you now know is going on behind the scenes of those of us who have lost a child? If so, I am truly sorry about that. I really am.

But please allow me one final chapter with some thoughts from pareavors.

If you haven't already observed, when child loss occurs, there are multiple losses going on. There is the loss of identity, the loss of future events, the loss of time spent together, the loss of that adult friendship whether it was already happening or a future dream, you can lose the personal future you had planned, you lose a sense of normalcy, and on and on it goes, including things like even the possible loss of a marriage.

> B.G.O.: *My daughter died 5 years ago. Her son (my grandson) & wife are due to have first child in march. (my first great grandchild) I'm so happy for them, but so sad my daughter isn't here. She's missing so much. My grandchildren don't have their mother here for all the milestones. I hurt for them. The pain never goes away. It gets softer at times but rages back when least expected.*
>
> B.A.: *...a year after I lost my daughter I was dating someone pretty seriously, and he had a drug addict son. His ex-wife told us that maybe I came into his life because they were going to lose their son. (Like associating with me was because their son was*

going to die.) It hurt me so much and needless to say, once the seed was planted our relationship deteriorated.

A.M.: It is particularly hurtful to me when comments come from my husband. Not only is he the father of my lost children, he's also my partner and is supposed to support me. In addition, he's trained on how to help and talk to people suffering from grief and in other forms of crisis as part of his job (he's in law enforcement). And he's very good at that job, but all his training and compassion fly right out the window when he gets home and sees his wife. His callous treatment of me has made me hate him.

Z.Q.: my precious son of 17 died 22 years ago and I still have 3 others but the memories are there, and still the pain of what if..................

L.P.S.: You grieve for all the memories you cannot have with each child you have lost.

P.S.C.G.: ...I lost my daughter also and I am raising her 2 small daughters along with help from my son...He loved his sister so much and is very good to her daughters...

P.U.: My brother lost his 5 year old daughter in an RTA 17 years ago. He still cannot stand to be in the house on his own.

G.C.: ...I constantly feel robbed of my daughter and all the life events she would've experienced. She would've been 25 this July. .. my sweet granddaughters grow up w/o their aunt (name). She was so full of life. I grieve for her. And all that would've been.

It is very difficult to be around people who do not understand the multi-faceted and never ending chain of losses we continually have to deal with, and because of that, our circle of friends can become quite small, causing even more pain.

A.M.H.: I let go of some family and friends because of their CONTINUED insensitivity and lack of acknowledging my extreme emotional and mental anguish. It was destroying me to have them in my life.

What Do I Do Now With This Information?

M.M.: I have intentionally denied FB friend requests from one woman who saw me a few months after my son passed and asked me if I was "over it" yet. Yeah, my feed isn't gonna be your style Honey. LOL
W.S.: ...You will find you lose many friends, they don't know how to act or what to say in your presence. I am raising my daughter's three children now. We all have good days as well as the bloody awful ones too. There are constant triggers and reminders.

It is also very difficult to be around people who don't understand that it is impossible to be the same person we were before our child was taken from this earth.

C.A.: I've changed forever and that's what people can't understand.
K.B.C.: ...you change after the loss of your child! I am not the same person I was before! EVERYTHING CHANGES!
E.N.: You have to find yourself all over again.
A.M.C.: I will never be the same person I was, something will be missing from my heart forever, a piece of me has died it feels like I have died but as I am sitting here typing I guess I haven't. I hate so much, so many people I hate I feel all I have left is hate.
MW.: When someone says you can put this behind you and move on, one would think they are talking about a bad financial decision instead of the life of your child. Idiots of ignorance.

So what do these things mean to you, the reader? It means you know three more specific areas where you can help us.

1. You can acknowledge to the grieving parent some of the extended chain of losses in their individual circumstance in the loss of their child (which puts you in that 5%).

2. You can be one of those who remain in our small circle of friends by not being distant or insensitive.
3. You now know and won't expect your friend or loved one who has experienced the death of a child to go back to being the person they were before a part of their very being was cut off from them (which can be a comfort and make you a "safe" person).

My prayer is that everyone who reads this book will be equipped to know how to truly be there for any pareavor who is either in their lives now, or will be in the future. And even more, that you will be part of growing that 5% into a much bigger number, as it should be.

Remember in the introduction when I asked you to pray, asking the Holy Spirit to speak to you as you immerse yourself into our world to show you what He wants you to see, and to do what He wants you to do? Please act on whatever that might be. Don't talk yourself out of it, or allow yourself to once again have good intentions, but no action. We need you.

We *need* you.

We need *you*!

POSTLUDE

Here is something I find rather interesting. There aren't many things in life that are so painful we would *never ever* want anyone else to experience it. But every pareavor I have ever met feels this way. It doesn't seem to matter how much we don't like someone (even hate…) we would never want them to go through the pain of losing a child.

C.A.: It's a feeling you never want people to understand.
C.S.: I would not wish losing a child on my worst enemy…

We are definitely a special and unique group of people. We are the "club" no one wants to be in, which comes with a life-long membership. But it isn't free. We have paid the ultimate price to be in it.

GPS Hope (Grieving Parents Sharing Hope) is a ministry my husband, Dave, and I started after the death of our Becca. We couldn't find many places that were offering hope to grieving parents. So much out there was telling us how we would never be the same, we would never get past our grief, and that life would no longer be worth living. After allowing God to bring us up and out beyond those words of hopelessness, we decided to be that hope for others who were searching for it the same way we were.

One night around 2 years after Becca's death, I woke up with a book title and a list of chapters rolling around in my spirit. I got up and wrote it all down, and began writing the book *When Tragedy Strikes: Rebuilding Your Life With Hope and Healing after the Death of a Child*. It is based on my journey out of the black pit of grief back into light and hope after losing our daughter, extending the tools God gave me to other grieving parents on the path behind us. My plan was to self-publish it, but apparently God had other plans. Through what I believe to be a Divine connection, I met David Hancock, the founder of Morgan James Publishing. He asked me to send what I had written so far, and 5 weeks later I found myself being offered a book contract. As of the writing of this book, *When Tragedy Strikes* is in the publishing process and will be available in bookstores everywhere July of 2016.

I highly recommend checking it out, and even purchasing a copy for yourself, and one for a pareavor you might know. However, if you give the book away, please let them know that it is for them to have *whenever they are ready to read it*. When the grief is still very fresh, often times a gift like this can feel like someone is telling them, "This will help you get over it." Nothing could be further from the truth, and it could easily just add to their pain, putting you in the category of being insensitive and no longer in their safe circle of friends. Use what you learned within the pages you just read to guide you in things like this.

Siblings can get lost in the process of grief. The parents are in their own world of blackness, and for quite a while struggle with being capable of being there for the other children. At the same time, many friends and family will inquire of the siblings how the parents are doing with their loss – totally bypassing the fact of the devastating loss the siblings themselves are suffering. Grandparents are another group that get lost in it all. They have a double whammy of losing their legacy and relationship with their precious grandchild, plus they have to watch their adult child go through such darkness and immense pain.

With this in mind, I have put together a book titled *From Ring Bearer to Pallbearer: Giving a Voice to Bereaved Siblings and Grandparent*. Where did this title come from? Well, our youngest son realized he was the ring bearer for his sister's wedding at age six, and then ten years later was the pallbearer for her casket at age sixteen.

Our three sons, both of Dave's parents, and my parents contributed to the writing of this book, and it is **available exclusively through GPS Hope. To get a FREE digital copy of this book**, go to the member page at www.gpshope.org. Sign up for our free members' library, and you will have instant access to the book, along with several other free items.

Also on www.gpshope.org, pareavors will be able to find articles and videos that will bring encouragement and hope. Occasional special events will be posted here as well. These events are specific times for pareavors to come together with others who understand, who can shed tears with one another, and lift each other up. And there is a page of resources, sharing other websites that offer items which can be purchased for pareavors. (Things that can bring us comfort and items that show us you still remember and honor the life of our child.)

After checking it out, please pass this information along to anyone who might find it useful, along with our Facebook page which can be found at www.facebook.com/groups/GPSHope.

One last thing: If *Come Grieve Through Our Eyes* has opened your eyes and given you a better understanding of what we are dealing with after the death of our child and how you can help us, maybe you can do me and other pareavors a huge favor. Let others around you know how important it is to help those of us who are so fragile come to a place of light and hope and life after the death of our child. You could even be someone who helps grow that 5% by blessing a couple of people with their own copy.

I give you a standing ovation for having a heart for this deep and heavy subject and for reading this book. Everyone's time is very valuable, and you have chosen to use several hours of your time to enter into our world, to find out what very few people want to know, and to learn how to be one of the rare friends who holds us up and keeps us going, helping us to heal and come to a place of hope and life again.

May God richly bless you as you go forward in the gift of life He has given you!

My New Normal

Author Unknown

Normal is having tears waiting behind every smile when you realize someone important is missing from all the important events in your family's life.

Normal is trying to decide what to take to the cemetery for Birthdays, Christmas, Thanksgiving, New Years, Valentine's Day, July 4th.

Normal is feeling like you can't sit another minute without getting up and screaming, because you just don't like to sit through anything anymore.

Normal is not sleeping very well because a thousand what if's and why didn't I's go through your head constantly.

Normal is reliving that day continuously through your eyes and mind, holding your head to make it go away.

Normal is having the TV on the minute you walk into the house to have noise, because the silence is deafening.

Normal is every happy event in my life always being backed up with sadness lurking close behind, because of the hole in my heart.

Normal is staring at every boy who looks like he is my son's age. And then thinking of the age he would be now. Then wondering why it is even important to imagine it, because it will never happen.

Normal is telling the story of my child's death as if it were an everyday, common place activity, and then seeing the horror in someone's eyes at how awful it sounds. And yet realizing it has become a part of my "normal."

Normal is having some people afraid to mention my child.

Normal is making sure that others remember her.

Normal is weeks, months, and years after the initial shock, the grieving gets worse sometimes, not better.

Normal is not listening to people compare anything in their life to this loss, unless they too have lost a child. Nothing — even if your child is in the remotest part of the earth away from you — it doesn't compare. Losing a parent is horrible, but having to bury your own child is unnatural.

Normal is sitting at the computer crying, sharing how you feel with chat buddies who have also lost a child.

Normal is feeling a common bond with friends on the computer in the UK or US but yet never having met any of them face to face.

Normal is a new friendship with another grieving mother, talking and crying together over our children and our new lives.

Normal is not listening to people make excuses for God. "God may have done this because..." I know that my child is in heaven, but hearing people trying to think up excuses as to why my child was taken from this earth is not appreciated and makes absolutely no sense to this grieving mother.

Normal is wondering this time whether you are going to say you have two children, because you will never see this person again and it is not worth explaining that my eldest child is in heaven. And yet when you say you have only two children to avoid that problem, you feel horrible as if you have betrayed your child.

Normal is asking God why he took your child's life and asking if there even is a God.

Normal is knowing I will never get over this loss, in a day or a million years.

And last of all, Normal is hiding all the things that have become "normal" for you to feel, so that everyone around you will think that you are "normal."

If you would like a digital copy of this to print out or to share on social media, please go to our free library at www.gpshope.org.

About the Author

Laura Diehl, along with her husband, Dave, lives in Southern Wisconsin. They are the founders of GPS Hope: Grieving Parents Sharing Hope, which extends hope and healing to all grieving parents through a growing list of resources and a loving community to encourage one another in their unique, difficult journey. She is also the author of the book *When Tragedy Strikes: Rebuilding Your Life With Hope and Healing After the Death of Your Child*, which will be available in bookstores in July of 2016.

Laura has also written *Triple Crown Transformation* (published in 2015), which is based on her many tragic life experiences, to help others learn the lessons she has been taught in three areas: See the Crown, Wear the Crown, Be the Crown. This book is the foundation of Crown of Glory Ministries, also founded by Dave and Laura, which encourages and equips the body of Christ to find their rightful royal place in God's kingdom.

"Kidz Korner" is a monthly article published for Impact Ministries International, written by Laura for children. It is based on her many years of children's ministry experience, encouraging kids to go deeper in their relationship with the Holy Spirit.

Laura loves to travel, which is good because she has traveled as an ordained minister for many years both nationally and internationally. She is available as an author, speaker, minister, and teacher and can be contacted by email at laura@crownofgloryministries.org.

More information about GPS Hope or Crown of Glory Ministries can be found in the Resource section.

About GPS Hope
(Grieving Parents Sharing Hope)

GPS Hope is a place for those who are going through the deep dark blackness of losing a child, to find encouragement and strength. It is a safe place for the shattered hearts of pareavors to take off their masks and be allowed to grieve as needed.

When Dave and Laura became pareavors, they didn't know anyone who had lost a child, could not find any local support groups for parents who were grieving the loss of a child (a different kind of grief than any other) and were left trying to navigate through the suffocating grief on their own.

Many books Laura read left her remaining in the place of hopelessness and despair, and seemed to indicate it was a land of no return. That just wasn't acceptable to her. There had to be a way to stop the intense stabbing pain that left one unable to function for months and years; a way to move forward, not just as a shell of a person waiting to die, but a survivor with something to give, and a full life to live.

There had to be a way to honor their daughter with life, not more death.

Their faith in God and belief in His ability to give them that life, pulled Dave and Laura out of that deep black pit that pareavors know all too well. That same faith in God has led them to where they are now, and where they continue to walk, one day at a time. They have learned to persevere and push past the tragic event, going beyond hope, to a place with fullness of purpose and meaning.

GPS Hope was birthed because Dave and Laura Diehl believe this is possible for *all* pareavors. It exists to give direction to hope, healing, and light, by offering various "tools" and resources to this unique group of parents.

RESOURCES

www.gpshope.org

On the GPS Hope website, you will be able to access the following (some of them are in the free members' library):
- *From Ring Bearer to Pallbearer: Giving a Voice to Bereaved Siblings and Grandparents* (**a book offered exclusively from GPS Hope**)
- A PDF of Joy scriptures and Hope scriptures
- A list of recommended books for grieving parents
- Occasional video messages
- Dates and information for occasional video chats
- Dates and information for occasional GPS Hope events (get-away retreats, etc.)
- Other miscellaneous items

https://www.facebook.com/groups/GPSHope
www.crownofgloryministries.org
www.facebook.com/crownofgloryministries.laura

REFERENCES

Chapter 1

[1]
http://www.ncbi.nlm.nih.gov/pmc/articles/PMC2841012/#R25

https://www.psychologytoday.com/blog/media-spotlight/201302/when-parent-loses-child

http://www.allpsychologycareers.com/topics/loss-of-a-child.html

Facing the Ultimate Loss: Coping with the Death of a Child by Robert J. Marx and Susan Wengerhoff Davidson

Made in the USA
San Bernardino, CA
04 March 2016